WAR
—— IS ——
PERSONAL

Hell, Luck, and Resilience:

A WWII Combat Marine's Accounts
of Okinawa and China

ROY WILKES, USMC
COMPILED BY ELAINE WILKES

"

Life is a crap shoot.
Roll the dice and know it's
all gonna be okay.

- Roy G. Wilkes

Paperback:	978-0-9774287-7-9
Hard Cover:	978-1-7334216-3-8
Large Print:	978-1-7334216-1-4
Audiobook:	978-1-7334216-8-3
Ebook:	978-1-7334216-4-5
CDs:	978-1-7334216-2-1

Library of Congress Control Number: 2019907870

Permission to use interviews from:
Bob Zimmerman's interview with Roy from his WWII documentary, *Rise of the Valiant,* razfilms.com

U.S. Marine Corps History Division, Oral History Branch

- Photos courtesy of U.S. Marine Archives

First printing edition 2019.
Golden Ratio Publishing
www.ElaineWilkes.com

WAR IS PERSONAL

Table of Contents

INTRODUCTION

ROY'S WRITINGS

Why Write This?

OLD PEOPLE THINK their memories are of interest to others .
. . they are not.

So I will write for myself.

Why write about things half forgotten?
Why write about a war that no one cares about,
or isn't interested in?

My memories are not about heroics.
I do not glorify myself because to even intimate
that I was heroic would be a lie.
The opposite is closer to the truth.
I was scared shitless.

Then why write?

Because these stories have to be told.

On Okinawa, I had the rare opportunity to see different forms
of combat.
I was in the middle of it, and not by choice.
For some reason, it just seemed to happen that way.
Time and again I ended up in very dangerous situations, and
always, barely, escaped.
The writings are about those escapes.

Some tragic, some funny, some interesting.
But all true.
They are written so someday someone might say,
"What an interesting life. God must have really loved him."

How the Marines Made Their Way to Okinawa

FROM DECEMBER 7, 1941, until May of the following year, the armed forces of the Empire of Japan freely carved a bloody swath across the Pacific, not simply to continue the empire's predatory, ten-year war against China, but to initiate an expanded war of aggression that involved the U.S. naval base at Pearl Harbor, Hawaii, and bases and cities in the American Commonwealth of the Philippines; the U.S. territory of Guam; British Burma and British Hong Kong; British Borneo; the Dutch East Indies and Dutch Borneo; British Singapore and the British Solomon Islands; Dutch Bali; the British Andaman Islands in the Bay of Bengal; and Dutch Java.

In mid-February 1942, British forces at Singapore surrendered, and in late February, the U.S. Navy suffered defeat in the Battle of the Java Sea. In April, U.S. and Filipino forces surrendered at Bataan, the Philippines.

But even as all this unfolded, President Franklin Roosevelt took the first steps to Allied victory. In March 1942, he named Admiral Chester Nimitz commander in chief of the U.S. Pacific Theater. In April, General Douglas MacArthur, who had been hastily evacuated from the Philippines, assumed control of U.S. forces in the Southwest Pacific Theater.

The Japanese military, though potent and highly motivated, was vulnerable. It reeled from an unexpected May 1942, naval defeat in the Battle of the Coral Sea, and absorbed an even worse body blow in the June 1942, naval Battle of Midway. In what would turn out to be Japan's undoing, the empire decided after Midway to wage a defensive war, and retain real estate already conquered. Japan was preparing to back itself into a war of attrition. Combining military strategy with a practical sense of political and logistical realities, the two American commanders devised an advance across the Pacific, moving west and northwest, island to island, with the home islands of Japan as the ultimate prize.

Because Japanese defenders were extraordinarily well dug-in on a multitude of Pacific islands, and not inclined to surrender, Nimitz and MacArthur (later joined by Vice Admiral William F. Halsey) elected to save time—and countless American, Japanese, and indigenous lives—by "leapfrogging" islands (such as Truk, in the Carolines) that, though firmly in Japanese hands, could be bypassed without harm to the overall Allied strategy.

The names of islands that were chosen for U.S. and Allied landings still speak to us with echoes of brutality and bravery: **New Britain**, Bismarck Archipelago (January – February 1942); **Guadalcanal**, Solomon Islands (August 1942 - February 1943); **Buna-Gona**, New Guinea (November 1942 - January 1943); **New Georgia**, Solomon Islands (June – August 1943); **Bougainville**, Solomon Islands (November 1943 – August 1945); **Makin** and **Tarawa**, Gilbert Islands (November 1943); **New Britain**, Solomon Islands (December 1943 – January 1944); **Kwajalein**, Marshall Islands (January – February 1944); **Saipan**, Mariana Islands (June - July 1944); **Guam**, Mariana Islands (July – August 1944); **Tinian**, Mariana Islands (July - August 1944); **Peleliu**, Palau Islands (September – November 1944); **Leyte**, the Philippines (October - December 1944); **Mindoro**, the Philippines (December 1944); **Iwo Jima,** Nanpo Shoto Islands (February – March 1945).

Then: April 1, 1945, brought the final (and largest) American amphibious landing, at Okinawa, Ryuku Islands.

Casualties were heavy throughout the island-hopping campaign. On Iwo Jima alone, the Marines sustained **24,000** casualties that included more than **6,000** killed. About **20,000** Japanese troops died there.

But the twelve-week toll at Okinawa was the worst: **45,000** American casualties, with **12,500** killed. About **100,000** Japanese died there, and an equal number of Okinawan civilians.

For a time, this was Roy Wilkes' world.

CHAPTER ONE

Spring Rain

IT RAINED THAT Spring.
But this was like no other Spring rain . . .
This rain was different.
The clouds were dark, low, and constant.
The rain lasted, and for some, it lasted forever.
Continuous rain dampens the soul.
The low, thick, dark clouds made sure God did not see.
What happened here was a secret from Him.
God was busy someplace else.
So this part of His universe went insane.
When the world goes mad, rain and mud are necessary.
Flowers and real spring rains are for other times.

Now we must play at war.
Real wars are fought in rain, in mud, during dark days and phosphorus-lit nights.

Make-believe wars are fought in the bright light of day, on dry ground,

with blue skies.
In make-believe wars men die in slow motion,
with adagio-type movements,
with memorable last words about home and loved ones.
Here men die suddenly, swiftly, silently, afraid.
The only constant is how fast their faces turn gray.
Everyone fears they will be next.
Yet when fear becomes reality, the expected is always such a surprise.
You pray to see the blue sky before you get surprised.

The rain is between a downpour and a drizzle.

It is constant.

Days drag into weeks.

It continues.

Men die, it rains on them.
The rain respects neither living nor dead.
It bloats everything.
The earth objects and refuses to accept any more.
The new lakes turn into seas of mud.
Not garden variety mud, but knee-deep slime.

And the rain continues.

The sound of constant shell fire mixes with the sound of thunder.
Occasional thunder, but always rain and fear.

No rainbow at the end.
No ending, just the rain.
You take it to your grave.

Forty years later at a Barry Manilow concert,
you spread a blanket on a grassy hillside.
Barry sings, "I made it through the rain."

Unfortunately, no one really makes it through the rain.
Not like the song.
We all died there.
Only some were buried sooner.
Those buried later . . . thought,
Talked, and wrote . . . about the rain . . . to themselves.

[OFFICIAL U.S. MARINE CORPS PHOTO BY STAFF SGT. J. J. CONNELLY]

SEA-GOING ARTILLERY: A 6th Marine Division 105 mm howitzer is in water several feet deep due to heavy and persistent rains on Okinawa. The sturdy crew of the Leathernecks continue to shell the Japanese, though every time the piece is fired, they are splattered with mud and water. (*Leatherneck is a military slang term for a U.S. Marine. The stiff, four-inch-high, leather neck-piece was part of the Marine Corps uniform from 1798 until 1872. In combat, it protected the neck and jugular vein from cutlasses slashes. On parade, it kept a Marine's posture erect.*)

[OFFICIAL U.S. MARINE CORPS PHOTO BY CORPORAL L.V. EASTMAN]

JAPANESE ALLY: The island was tactically "secured" but rivers of mud conspired with die-hard Japanese to make mopping-up a rugged business on Okinawa. It's taking a tractor to pull this ammunition trailer out of the waist-deep waters.

[OFFICIAL U.S. MARINE CORPS PHOTO BY PVT. BOB BAILEY]

OKINAWA MUD: On VE Day the Marines on Okinawa were rushing their men and supplies to the front through the morass of mud on the roads caused by all day rains. The soldiers and Marines of the Tenth Army were giving no rest to the enemy troops holding the line protecting Naha, the capital city, and the southern area of the island.

[OFFICIAL U.S. MARINE CORPS PHOTO BY CORPORAL JOHN CURRAN]

ESCAPE: Knee deep in the water's edge along the seawall on Okinawa, a Japanese soldier makes an attempt to escape from pursuing Marines. One enemy soldier lies in the mud, killed by the Leathernecks.

CHAPTER TWO

THE THOUSAND YARD STARE

I FIRST NOTICED it one night when we were moving up to the front lines.
We were walking on a narrow path.
Men coming off the front lines were on the opposite side.
Nobody was talking. We were just quietly passing each other.
The men on the opposite side looked tired, unshaven, and dirty.

But there was something else about them that seemed strange.
I thought, somehow they look different than us.
There were no smiles, no wisecracks—
just silence as we passed each other.
I thought, for some strange reason, they all look alike.

Then it dawned on me. It's the eyes.
When they look at you, they seem to be looking beyond you.
They never blink . . .
They just stare off at something in the distance.
All of them do the same thing.

Their eyes are different.
It's kind of scary to look at them.

Later I learned it had a name.
They called it "the thousand-yard stare."

Soon I caught it without knowing it.
Maybe your mind is so preoccupied that something happens to your eyes.
Eventually you get rid of it, but sometimes it returns.

The thousand-yard stare was a way of shutting down.
It made your face emotionless.
It left you alone with your thoughts and waking nightmares.
Actually, I really don't know what happens inside you when you have it.
It's just there.
Days of combat will give it to you.
That's the only way you can get it.
You cannot fake it.
It's just there.
It brings silence with it.
I think the brain shuts down and that reflects in the eyes.
You stare at nothing, you see nothing, you think nothing.
You become a zombie and your eyes reflect it.
You lose your personality.
Welcome to the thousand-yard club.

Record Levels of Mental Breakdown

"MORE MENTAL HEALTH issues arose from the Battle of Okinawa than any other battle in the Pacific during World War II. The constant bombardment from artillery and mortars coupled with the high casualty rates led to a great deal of personnel coming down with combat fatigue (post-traumatic stress disorder).

Additionally, the rains caused mud that prevented tanks from moving and tracks from pulling out the dead, forcing Marines (who pride themselves on burying their dead in a proper and honorable manner) to leave their comrades where they lay.

This, coupled with thousands of bodies both friend and foe littering the entire island, created a scent you could nearly taste. Morale was dangerously low by the month of May and the state of discipline on a moral basis had a new low barometer for acceptable behavior.

The ruthless atrocities by the Japanese throughout the war had already brought on an altered behavior (deemed so by traditional standards) by many Americans resulting in the desecration of Japanese remains, but the Japanese tactic of using the Okinawan people as human shields brought about a new aspect of terror and torment to the psychological capacity of the Americans."

—Sgt. Rudy R. Frame, "Okinawa: The Final, Great Battle of World War II"
(Reprinted from the Marine Corps Gazette with permission; Copyright © October 2012 MCA&F www.mca-marines.org)

CHAPTER THREE

MOVE UP

THOSE WERE HIS last words: "Move up." He was telling me that there was too much space between me and the Marine in front of us. Maybe the Marine in front of me was ten to fifteen feet away. The interval should have been about twelve feet. Maybe more. Maybe less. There were no hard and fast rules. No exact measurement.

Bobbie was suddenly alongside me, telling me to move up. He was too close to me. The safeties on our M1's were off. We expected a firefight. Once the firefight started, there would be no time to push the safety and get off a shot.

The group of us were in the front of the lines. I do not know why we were out there. I do not know what we were looking for. It doesn't work that way in the Marine Corps. No one owes you an explanation. You are told to "move out" and you go. It's that simple.

In number, we were less than a platoon and more than a squad.

We just got a new lieutenant that morning. For some unknown reason, he was up at the point.

We were spread in a single line in a narrow Okinawa valley with slight hills on both sides. I don't know why we were on the low ground instead of the high ground. I am not a military strategist, but it seemed dumb to be down there.

Then it happened.

The entire side of the hill on our left seemed to raise fifty feet in the air . . . a tremendous . . . explosion . . . smoke . . . rocks . . . tons of dirt . . . all in the air . . . impossible to see. I was thrown forward. As I went forward my rifle also went forward and my finger pressed the trigger.

I awoke and Bobbie was about five feet in front of me . . . my rifle was several feet away.

A strange thing happened. I could see that my rifle had fired because the shell casing hadn't ejected. The rifle bolt went forward and the casing was jammed between the bolt and the breech. I was half buried by dirt and rocks. My helmet had been blown off.

Bobbie made no sound. He was turning a gray color. I had seen that too often . . . he was either dead, or dying.

There was another Marine in back of me. I couldn't turn to see him. No sound from him either.

All twenty-three Marines in front of us were completely buried. The air was filled with dust. I couldn't see more than ten feet. I had no idea what happened. I wasn't hurt, just buried in dirt and rocks.

The Japs started to lay in a barrage. Shells started exploding all around us. I was not alert enough to tell if they were mortars or artillery. The shelling didn't last long.

I lay there.

I could not reach Bobbie.

I didn't even want to try to dig myself out.

I was still in a daze when I saw four Marines running through the dust, carrying a stretcher. I recognized two of them. One was a Navy corpsman. The other was Barber, a tough Marine with a fierce handlebar mustache. He looked and acted like a Marine you would see in the movies. They came to me and started digging me out. I told them I was okay and asked them to try to help Bobbie. They started to dig around him. They dug out his arm, stuck a rifle in the ground, and started to give him blood plasma. They couldn't find out what was wrong with him. When they got to Bobbie's waist, they removed his cartridge belt. Then they saw a .30 caliber round that had gone through a clip of ammunition in his cartridge belt and then through his side. Bobbie died then, or he'd already been dead for a few minutes.

The corpsman and Barber stopped working on him and dug me out and dug out the guy in back of me. That guy was still alive.

They asked me if I could walk. I said, "Yes."

Barber said, "Show me. Walk over there." He pointed to a place a few feet away. I walked. One guy said something was wrong with my legs. Another said, "Let's get the guy in back on a stretcher and get the hell out of here."

The man who'd been behind me was still alive but unconscious. I don't know his name.

I looked at Bobbie and I remember saying, or maybe just thinking, "Bobbie, I'll live for the both of us." I doubt if that act of generosity really impressed Bobbie.

The four Marines carried the stretcher and told me to run with them. We stopped in back of a wall. There was an open space in front of us. The Marines said it was a sniper's lane. They threw a phosphorus grenade that caused a lot of smoke. While the smoke clouded the open space, they ran with the stretcher to cover behind the next wall.

All of a sudden, I didn't care to run anymore . . .

As I walked through the opening I could hear sniper fire. I didn't care if I got hit. I walked the rest of the way back to the lines. When I got there, a medic put a large colored tag around my neck and told me to go back to the Battalion First Aid to get medical attention. Battalion First Aid was another couple hundred yards in back of the lines.

I walked a short distance and then I sat down on the steps of an

Okinawan tomb and started to cry.

A column of Marines was moving up on the small path toward the front. They all glanced over and saw me sitting there crying. I guess they thought I was a coward or that I had cracked up. I couldn't explain to them that I had been beyond where they were going. I had been to hell and back . . . I had just killed my best friend . . . I had seen everyone in the squad but me and one other guy get killed. I never did find out what happened to the guy in back of me.

I didn't do anything heroic. I was just there. I was just a witness to the war. The story ends there. Sure, I went back to Battalion First Aid and got tended to.

Later, I got the Purple Heart for wounds received in action.

I found out later that the lieutenant had thrown a grenade into a cave filled with explosives and chemicals. The explosion decapitated him. He lasted less than one day on the front lines.

I recalled when Bobbie and I shared a pup tent. We were in the rear area before being committed to the Naha section of the fighting. Bobbie looked at me and shared one of his profound seventeen-year-old thoughts. He said, "Roy, I was just thinking. If one of us had to get killed . . . you know, if it had to be either you or me . . . I would much prefer it to be you."

Bobbie was honest and funny.

[OFFICIAL U.S. MARINE CORPS PHOTO BY PFC JOHN T. SMITH]

PUSHING ON: In deployed order the Leathernecks of Major General Pedro Del Valle's First Marine Division advance over a hill against the Japanese forces constricted in the southern part of the island. The men near the crest keep low to avoid outlining themselves against the skyline. Each Marine keeps his trigger finger ready and a wary eye searching for any signs of the enemy.

CHAPTER FOUR

NUTHIN' BUT DEATH AHEAD

THERE ARE NO taps . . .

No folded flag presented to the next of kin.

No long goodbyes.

No memorable last words.

He just stepped off the edge of the world . . . into nothing.

Someone would miss him, but not here, not now.

He was gone and there was nothing I could do but run and leave him to eternity.

Leave him with a bullet through his cartridge belt and through him.

His rifle stuck in the ground with a plasma bottle on it.

The medic turned to another wounded.

No more help for Bobbie. It was too late for him.

The corpsman just turned away and went to the other wounded men.

Not a word.

No goodbye.

War is business.

Death is the end of that business, and it means Bobbie lost his war.

One of the thousands who lost his battle with war.

Just leave him down there, half buried, helmet off.
He turned that terrible gray color of death.
No rest in peace.
No Bible verse.
No Mass.
Just death.
That's all he had.
Run back to the front lines.
How strange to run back to the front.
There is nothing but death ahead of the front lines.
During World War I they called it "No Man's Land."
That is the area between the two front lines. No one owns it yet.
No one lives there for very long.
Try to get out of harm's way, when they keep putting you there.
How many times can you survive?
On several occasions, I have been in it.
On each occasion men died and were wounded.
Every time they died for nothing—not honor, not country, not
the Corps.

Fifty years later I would realize how terribly dumb and stupid
the whole idea of war is.
But not now, not today.
Those thoughts come with time and reflection.

Now, like a trapped animal, the only instinct is to stay alive a little
longer.
For what?

So I could stay alive for another look at death;

So that I could escape again and look at it again.
Until it was over.
But no one told me it was over.
No one said that death was no longer trying to get me.

Years later I realized I beat it.
The grim reaper missed me.
The dumb bastard had a close-up swing at me on six different occasions
—and missed.
Well, he came close enough to give me the Purple Heart, but even that's considered a miss.

I heard the line in a song . . . "Stayin' alive . . . stayin' alive."
It is so simple.
War is so simple.
That is what war is all about.
Not killing the enemy.
Not heroics, just "stayin' alive."
Do that and you have found the secret to war.

Try to get out of harm's way when they keep putting you there.

How many times can you survive?

Only till you get overconfident, then it comes as a surprise.

He gets you. We all end that way. He eventually gets you.

The Battle of Okinawa
1 April 1945 (Easter Sunday) – 22 June 1945

PFC WILKES FOUND himself in the Pacific, on a Japanese-held island called Okinawa. Seventy miles long, fewer than ten miles across, and just 350 miles from Japan. Okinawa was the last stop on America's ambitious island-hopping campaign of World War II.

"The battle has been referred to as the "typhoon of steel" in English, or tetsu no bofu ("violent wind of steel") in Japanese. The nicknames refer to the ferocity of the fighting, the intensity of kamikaze attacks from the Japanese defenders, and to the sheer numbers of allied ships and armored vehicles that assaulted the island."

- WorldWarPhotos.com

BEGINNING IN APRIL 1945, American and Japanese men fought and killed each other as never before. Caught in the crossfire between these warring powers were the native inhabitants of Okinawa.

"Over **250,000** people lost their lives. Approximately **150,000** Okinawans, about a third of the population, perished. At the battle's end, somewhere between a third and half of all surviving civilians were wounded. No battle during the Second World War, except Stalingrad, had as massive a loss of civilian life. The Japanese, determined to fight to the last man, almost achieved their objective, but in defeat **100,000** Japanese combatants died rather than surrendered. In the end, fewer than **10,000** of General Mitsuri Ushijimas's Thirty-Second Army were taken prisoner.

"At least **100,000** civilians were either killed in combat or were ordered to commit suicide by the Japanese military."

- Encyclopedia Britannica

"MOST JAPANESE TROOPS and Okinawa citizens believed Americans took no prisoners and they'd be killed on the spot if captured. As a result, countless took their own lives too.

To encourage their surrender, General Buckner initiated propaganda warfare and dropped millions of leaflets declaring the war was all but lost for Japan.

About **7000** Japanese soldiers surrendered, but many chose death by suicide. Some jumped from high hills, others blew themselves up with grenades."

- History.com

CHAPTER FIVE

LISTEN

DURING ALL OF that training, no one ever said anything about the noise. Not one person talked about the most important thing on the battlefield: the different sounds. It is the sounds that determine your fate.

The sound of an incoming shell is different from the sound of an outgoing shell.

The sound of a shell that will land close is different from the sound of a shell that will land a safe distance away.

The sound of a large incoming shell is much different than the sound of a small shell. Incoming mortar shells do not make a noise.

The ears are the first line of defense, yet no one in training mentions how important it is to sort out all the sounds. Artillery sounds like thunder.

The yell, "Incoming!" is of life-and-death importance. Who yells it is also important. If some veteran yells it . . . hit the deck. If a recruit yells it . . . he could make you look stupid.

Sounds during the night are uniquely important. No one really sleeps. You learn to sleep and listen . . . a habit you keep for the rest of your life.

[OFFICIAL U.S. MARINE CORPS PHOTO FROM MARINE ARCHIVES]

LACEWORK: Japanese night raiders are greeted with a lacework of anti-aircraft fire by the Marine defenders of Yontan airfield on Okinawa. In the foreground, silhouetted against the interlaced paths of tracer bullets, were Marine Corsair fighter planes of the "Hell's Belles" squadron.

OKINAWA, MAY 11, 1945: Harassing fire directed towards Jap positions in Southern Okinawa begins during the early morning hours of May 11, 1945, as an all-out offensive gets underway to dislodge Japanese positions on Southern Okinawa.

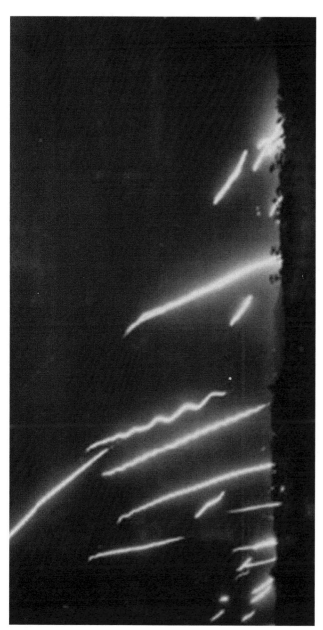

[OFFICIAL U.S. MARINE CORPS PHOTO BY STAFF SGT. DAVID PEAKIN]

SCENE ON OKINAWA: The projectiles from the various weapons of the Japanese and Marines form a pattern of irregular and wavy lines in the night on southern Okinawa.

CHAPTER SIX

A TALE OF TWO FRIGHTENED PEOPLE

THE JAPANESE AND Okinawan women had been taught that the American Marines were subhuman. They believed that the Marines ate babies. They were terribly frightened of the Marines.

Before landing on Okinawa, the Marines were taught that the Okinawan women were exceptionally dangerous, and that they didn't care for their own lives. If given a chance, they would blow themselves up with a hand grenade and try to take several Marines with them. Soldiers and local men had to surrender dressed only in loincloths, with their hands raised. The women were allowed to stay dressed in their traditional ankle-length black kimonos. We were told that they would conceal a hand grenade in the folds of the kimono and were very dangerous. I wanted no part of old Okinawan women.

One day we met.

She was with a group of old women walking toward our lines. I happened to be at the front of a small group of Marines. She had something wrapped in a scarf. She made a bag out of the scarf and had something in it. I motioned to the other guys to stop. The old women were about fifteen yards away.

They stopped.

I motioned for the old lady to put down the scarf.

She just stared at me.

Again, I motioned. I knew that she knew what I wanted her to do, yet she refused.

I didn't want her to come any closer to me. We had a standoff until I took the safety off my rifle. She heard the click and knew that she would soon meet her ancestors.

She put down the scarf and the contents in it. I motioned for the rest of the group to start walking again. The guys in the rear could eventually search the women to make sure they weren't carrying hidden explosives. Now they passed their first test, they were not carrying any packages. They moved past me to the rear echelon.

Minus the package, the old woman looked very sad. They all looked frightened, tired, and panicky. But they were the lucky ones who had survived a terrible battle that killed over 200,000 Okinawan civilians and had lasted more than eighty days.

Now they had no idea of how they would be treated by these subhuman Marines. At least the first ones they met didn't shoot all of them.

After they left, I went up to the cloth package and poked it with my rifle. I was curious to see what she had been carrying for all those days. The cloth separated and I saw bright-colored cloth inside the wrapping. I saw a bright green and a bright pink kimono. This was very unusual because up to this time I had only seen Okinawans dressed in black.

I didn't feel badly about taking the kimonos away from the old lady because the thing they should have taught the ladies is that the Marines not only ate babies but were also great souvenir hunters. I put the kimonos in my backpack and carried them for the rest of the campaign.

Anyway, the woman would have only made it to the next line of Marines before one of them got two souvenirs.

CHAPTER SEVEN

Someone Wants To Kill You

YOU ARE ON patrol ahead of the front lines.

A year ago, I thought all Marines were the same.
They were all Marines, but with different jobs.

★ ☆ ★

Marines do a lot of things.
They unload boats.
They drive trucks.
They type reports.
They bury the dead.
They load ordnance on planes.
They fire large cannons.
They fire small cannons.
They fire mortars.
They staff hospitals.
They all carry rifles.
But less than five percent get a chance to be on the front lines and
actually use those rifles to fire at the enemy.

You were stupid enough to be in that small minority.

Your senses are more alert than they have ever been because you either pay attention now, or you could get hurt, or die.

Someone may think that the task at hand is to kill the Japs.
You don't care if the Japs live or die.
You are a reluctant warrior.
You are not mad at anyone.
You do not want to save America from the dirty Jap.
You would like to be someplace else . . . anyplace but here.

How the hell did you get involved in this?

It all happened so fast. You joined the Marines because
your brother was a Marine.
You should've devoted more thought to the entire matter.
Now you really are in harm's way.
That means someone is trying to kill you.
Dammit, now pay attention. Your mind is wandering and that cannot happen out here. You pay a big price for not paying attention.

Your only interest is to stay alive during this patrol.
Selfish but true.
Save the brave stuff for when you're an old man telling war stories in a bar.
Now you're a frightened teenager.

Singleness of purpose.

One purpose: stay alive.
Through all the types of combat you have lived through.

Just live another hour, another day, and another patrol.

At any minute, Marines will die out here while others are driving
their trucks and doing their paperwork.
You resent that, but somebody must cook the meals, play in the
band, write for the paper, and just goof off in the rear area.
Yes, every Marine who was on Okinawa wasn't in combat.
All will have heroic stories to tell.

However, save all that resentment for later.
Right now, pay attention.
Someone wants to kill you.

Many years later, some songwriter described it perfectly.
"Stop, hey, what's that sound? Everybody look what's going down."
Pay attention to the sounds.
The sounds are the most important things out here.
Animals live by their sense of smell.
Frontline Marines live by their sense of hearing.

Just as shells make different sounds, a Marine Corps Browning
Automatic Rifle sounds entirely different than a Japanese Nambu
pistol.
Knowing the difference means you can tell if we are firing at them,
or if they are firing at us.
Just that little difference can cost you your life—or save it.

Okay, say you hear things, but you also have to know what to
look for.
Look, but be careful about what you see because your eyes
will betray you out here.
You have to be careful for your other Marines who are with you.
It is dangerous out here.
Do not make it more dangerous for them with your stupidity
and fear.

I wish I had known more about the various jobs in the Marine
Corps before I was a recruit.
Better yet, I wish I had known more about the various services
before I joined the Corps.
I would've joined the Coast Guard.

What does it take to stay alive?
Combat knowledge.
Intuition.
Knowledge of sounds.
Desire to live.
Luck.
And more luck.
The blessing of the good Lord.
Prayer.
The survivor sense of a trapped animal.
All of the above have to be working for you.
But you also have to pay attention and use all of the above.
If your mind wanders,
You're dead.
It's that simple.

It would be nice if at the end of the day you could relax, having

done your duty.

At nightfall, you share a hole with the buddy.

You sleep two and watch two.

Someone is sneaking through the lines and will kill you if you sleep, so you watch.

In the morning, you start all over again. Another day, another patrol, another sleepless night.

It goes on like that forever.

You never escape it. Even when the war is over, you remember.

Oh, God, how you remember.

You live through it, but you were tortured by it.

It comes back when you least expect it, but mostly at night.

CHAPTER EIGHT

ONE UPA REEP

MARTIAL MUSIC CAN make you proud to be a Marine.
The cadence of the drill sergeant: "One upa reep."
Who knows what that means, but somehow it makes sense.
Everybody marches to it. "One upa reep areep, areep, one upa areep."

No one owes you an explanation, all you need to know is that your left foot goes forward when you hear "areep."
See how simple life can be?
Move your left foot forward every time you hear this redneck yell "areep."
Do that and you are a Marine.

Southern talk seemed strange at first.
Now I am so used to it. I have begun to think that my last name is Shithead because I have heard "Wilkes, you shithead" so often I now respond to it.
I have actually thought about having ninety percent of my brain

removed so I would have something in common with the drill sarge.

I don't know if he was shot in the head and got that way, or if he was that way since birth.

CHAPTER NINE

No One Let Us Know It Was Over

No one blew a whistle or sounded a bugle to let us know it stopped.
There were no high fives and "we won" crap.
No celebration.
No women with bottles of wine waiting to kiss the victors.

The killing stopped because there was no one left to kill.
Old women and children surrendered now.
A few very old men mixed in with the lot.
The apprehension showed on all their frightened faces.
They still had to determine if the American Marines were as bad as they had been told.
We had no time to be nice to them.
We offered them nothing, just a nod of the head signaling them to move to the rear.

There was no "Let's give a little boy a pat on the head and a candy bar."

We kept a safe distance from them, fifteen to twenty feet. True or not, women could still be carrying grenades.

This was no time to let your guard down.
Let the rear echelon bother with the search of the women.
Right now, these people were in the way of killing.
Our only interest was to get them out of the way.
No compassion, no sympathy, no sadness for them. No joy that they surrendered and would live.
They were in the way.

We did not know how many Japanese soldiers were left.
No young men surrendered with the masses.
They surrendered individually and dressed only in a loin cloth.
There was never a mass surrender of Jap troops.

At the start, no one ever told us to be afraid, and at the end no one ever told us that it was all over.
Just as I don't remember when the rain stopped, and the spring turned to summer. So, instead of the corpses being soaked, bloated and buried in mud, they were bloated and burned black by the sun and covered with flies.

I do not remember when the killing stopped; gradually, imperceptibly, eventually.
But when the rain and the killing stopped, it no longer mattered.
We had all been wet and dead too long for it to matter.

There was never any talk of who died, or how they died.
Not now, or even later on Guam or in China.

It was as if they never existed, and Okinawa never happened.

I wonder if everyone else wanted to cry,
and at least visit the graves of those who died.
It would have been nice to say goodbye.
But there was no bugler blowing taps.
No ceremony.
No requiem.
No monuments.
No rest in peace.
There was just a lot of unfinished business.

CHAPTER TEN

THE UNEXPECTED
VISITOR

Time:	Christmas Eve 1945
Location:	Northeast China about seventy-five miles from the Manchurian border
Who:	About fifty Marines guarding railroad Bridge #54
Weather conditions:	Light snow falling, temperature about twenty degrees

There were no Christmas carols, no "God Rest Ye Merry Gentlemen," not one present for anyone, no Christmas tree.

We inherited our lieutenant from the motor pool while we were on Okinawa. He was not an infantry man and admitted he knew nothing about the infantry. Yet he was our leader. We all tolerated him. When the battle was over he reverted to being a prick. We continued to tolerate him, but now he expected to be obeyed.

Fifty of us lived in a wood barracks. The lieutenant and the sergeant lived in a small Quonset hut we erected for a mess hall.

The lieutenant decided that for Christmas any man who wanted to could go into the nearest small village and bring back to the barracks the whore of his choice for an evening. Naturally both the lieutenant and the sergeant also availed themselves of this privilege. A guess is that about twenty-five of the men brought back whores.

Those who did not take advantage of this gift had guard duty for the night. The revolution did not stop because the Marines were getting laid, so someone had to go into the snow and watch the bridge and guard the outside of the barracks. That was my station. I was walking around the barracks when I saw a light on the tracks. I heard a locomotive. We had never seen a locomotive operate at night. That was just too dangerous. The locomotive stopped at our barracks and a figure dressed as a Chinaman got off and said something in Chinese to the engineer.

I unslung my rifle pointed it at the figure and told him to get back on the locomotive and get the hell off Marine Corps property, or I would put a bullet up his ass.

The locomotive backed away, back down the tracks where it came from, and left the guy in the long dress standing there. I started to try to stop the engine but the engineer ignored me. The man who got off the engine had a long gray beard and seemed to be a white man, not Chinese. I told him that we shoot anything that comes inside the wire. The bridge was surrounded by concertina barbed wire piled three high. Every Chinese knew that only

Marines were allowed inside the wire. This guy started to walk toward me. I told him to halt and stay where he was. He stopped and held out his hands. He yelled that he was a Catholic priest and that he came to the most deserted outpost to say Mass and hear confessions. When I heard that I almost crapped. Odd things like this always happened to me in the Corps—like a priest showing up on Christmas Eve trying to do God's work. Little did he realize how much of God's work was ahead of him.

I told the priest not to move until I told the lieutenant he was here. I ran to the Quonset hut and knocked on the door. A voice from inside yelled, "What the hell do you want!" I said, "A Catholic missionary is here to say Mass and hear confessions." The lieutenant and sergeant thought it was a joke. They both got really angry with me through the closed door because this was the typical type of bad joke I was capable of. I pleaded with them that I wasn't joking, and asked one of them to open the door and take a look. I guess they were in the middle of pushy-pushy and didn't want to be bothered. When the sergeant opened the door to chew out a piece of my ass he saw the man standing in the snow about fifty yards away. The blood drained from his face because if it really was a priest, and he reported what was going on at this post, both he and the lieutenant would become privates overnight. All priests knew the higher ups. He said, "Wait here" and slammed the door. I heard a lot of activity inside. In a couple of minutes, he and the lieutenant were dressed and at the door. They told me to bring the priest in that door while they got the women out the opposite door.

I went back to fetch the priest. As he entered, I could hear the opposite door close. The operation went flawlessly. The women were outside in the snow and the big brave Marines couldn't have cared less. For the moment, their asses were still in the Corps and out of the brig. The lieutenant explained to the missionary that the barracks was off limits to everyone except the Marines, and that I would announce that there was a Catholic missionary here to say Christmas mass.

I left, went to the opposite door to get the two shivering Chinese, and told them they could go into the barracks with me. I made the announcement that the priest was on board and that went over like a turd on the church steps. The priest later heard confessions and said Mass. He encouraged all denominations to attend. The lieutenant and sergeant made sure he didn't leave the Quonset hut.

While in the barracks, I announced that the lieutenant said that all women must be out by sunup and walking to the next bridge, which was five miles away and guarded by the Japanese. Most of the men thought that was chicken shit and were certain the women wouldn't make the walk since they weren't dressed for it. I suggested that the guys talk it over with the lieutenant and sergeant. None of them took the opportunity to do so. Most of the men were afraid of what would happen to them if the colonel found out that we were running a brothel that night, instead of guarding a bridge. So the girls were on their way before sunup. Later, on Christmas Day, the lieutenant decided that the priest could go into the barracks. Every bed was made. The place was aired out. The men were standing by their beds trying not to look too guilty.

Just another day in the life of the brave Marine. No one could believe this stuff.

CHAPTER ELEVEN

ON COMING HOME

EVENTUALLY WE ALL came back to America.

We were a year late, but we were back on American shores.

There was no parade.

No welcome home signs.

No wives or girlfriends waiting on the dock.

It was a non-event.

Get off the ship.

Get in the trucks. Ride to the San Diego Marine recruit depot and wait.

We were told we were waiting for a train to take us to the Great Lakes Naval Station.

We would be discharged from there.

I was twenty years old.

I had fought in a World War and a revolution.

Not just participated, but was fired upon and saw men die.

I had seen more combat than most movie heroes will ever portray.

No, I was not a hero.

I was just a spectator.

I watched real heroes fight and die.
I saw enough of it to get the thousand-yard stare.
I saw enough of it to get a lifetime of memories.
I saw enough to become a haunted house.
Now I would go home.
When I got home I realized I was a year too late.
Everyone had exchanged war stories.
Actually, no one else had really been in combat.
They had been in the war, not combat.
So there was no one to tell what happened.
No one really wanted to hear what would sound like fabricated stories.
The truth sounded strange even to me.

I had no desire to tell them stories.
Actually, I had little to say because I was not a very good Marine.
My only goal was to live.
I did not desire to die for my country.
I did not resent or hate anyone.

In some strange way, I now miss the thunder of the howitzers, the shriek of the shells overhead, the mud, the rain.
I was more of a man then.

Now I'm a scared adult with nothing to be frightened of.
But now I'm so frightened, I shake.
I thought I shook because I was cold.
I don't know why, but I am so cold.
Someday I will figure it all out.
Now I have to be a clown.

CHAPTER TWELVE

THE PHONE BOOTH

About fifteen yards back from the main entrance of Medinah
Country Club
there is a soundproof telephone booth.
I first met the phone booth in 1947; it was the summer after I
returned
from the Marine Corps.
I thought I had adjusted well to being a civilian.
I had met someone who was a chorus girl at the Palmer House
in Chicago.
She lived with her wealthy parents in Oak Park.
Her father belonged to Medinah Country Club.

On July fourth, I was invited to go with the family for dinner and
fireworks at the country club.
After dinner, we adjourned to the front of the club to watch the
fireworks.

Then it happened!

You have all heard the sound of fireworks shooting high into the night sky.

The only thing wrong is that the sound is the exact sound a mortar makes.

In fact, they may even use mortars to shoot the fireworks.

I tried to ignore the sound.

That didn't work.

I panicked.

Now they were shooting two and three at a time.

I got up and excused myself and said I would be right back.

I went into the clubhouse . . .I could still hear the sound of the mortars.

By now I was really panicked. I had to get away from the sound.

It was the sound that haunted me.

That damn sound.

I saw the phone booth and got in and closed the large soundproof door.

There was a chair in there. I sat down and pretended that I was making a phone call.

No one was going to get me out of that phone booth while those damn mortars were going off.

After a while I saw my girlfriend looking for me.

I pretended to hang up the phone.

I told her about the important call I had to make.

She said, "You were frightened by the fireworks!"

I said, "Oh, no, why would that frighten anyone?"

I couldn't explain about the sound of the mortars.

Her parents thought I was a real jerk.

CHAPTER THIRTEEN

SYNTHETIC HEROES

When the battle was over the synthetic heroes emerged.
At first they exaggerated their battle experiences.
What they claimed was exaggerated. The horror, the killing, the
suffering were all exaggerated.

However, the biggest transgression was the fact that rear-echelon
troops boasted of completely imagined experiences.

It was over.
The shooting stopped.
The howitzers were silent.
We were safe a thousand miles from the danger.

I wanted to be much braver than I was, but the real heroes were
now resting in their neat graves, or they were cursing their bravery
in veteran's hospitals.

The truth is I was a coward.
I was frightened.

Not just scared, but really frightened. Twenty-four hours a day, seven days a week, for three months straight.
I never stopped being frightened.

Many years later, I will pretend that I was a Marine.
I was just a frightened boy in dungarees. Did that make me a Marine?
I don't think so.
I was unlucky enough to get a front row seat to war.
I was just a spectator.
I saw more than ninety-nine percent of servicemen see.
Now I claim credit for just being there,
not doing anything,
just being there and seeing war.

Now at night, when I see war I try to shake my head and make the pictures go away.
Maybe the pictures would be more welcome if I were doing heroic acts.

Now, many years later, I realize I should have carried Bobbie's body back with me.
I left him with his rifle barrel stuck into the ground with a plasma bottle hanging on it and the plastic line leading to his arm.

The corpsman said he was dead. I knew that from the gray complexion.
I did not know if I could make it, and I did not even think of carrying a dead body to slow me up.
I have carried Bobbie for fifty years.

It would have been easier to carry him that day.

I hear so often that the Marines never leave their dead behind.
Men who read books about Marine Corps tradition, and who have
never had the opportunity to leave a dead friend behind in order
to save themselves, believe that.

"They are dead. They cannot help you and you cannot help them.
It is over for them.
Now do what you can to save your own ass."
That is not in the grand tradition of the Corps.
Not all Marines are Marines.
Not all Marines are heroes.
Some of us were just spectators.
We were lookie-loos at war.
We never bought in to the grand traditions of the Corps because
we were too frightened to observe them.

CHAPTER FOURTEEN

SOUNDS LASTING A LIFETIME

IN ANCIENT TIMES a desperate plea and prayer was made by the Greek warrior Ajax while he fought on a darkened plain:

> *Father in heaven,*
> *Deliver us from darkness,*
> *And make our skies clear.*
> *If we must die,*
> *Let us die in the light.*

Two thousand years later, less poetic men felt the same prayer without putting it into words. They hoped to see the sun before dying. Surely they all would die, but to die in the warm, dry light of the sun was a comforting thought.

Dark clouds and rain had reflected the sound and pressure of constant howitzer fire for three weeks. To the novice, it was difficult to distinguish the rolling barrage of cannon from the rolling rumble of thunder. They were both there, but the trained ear of the young warrior could make the life and death decision of every type of sound. "Outgoing!" . . . "Incoming!" . . . were words and thoughts that classified the direction and intention of every sound. There was a sequence to the sound. First, the distant rolling like thunder. Then came the sequenced sound of the overhead shots. Finally, the explosions. All in the same rapid-fire sequence. Sometimes the sound sequencing got confusing. Too many rounds to make out the sequence of thunder, whiz, and boom. Too many artillery batteries firing rapid fire to make the proper distinctions. But the memory of the sounds will remain with them for the rest of their lives.

Forty years later, while playing the first hole of the beautiful No. 6 golf course in Pinehurst, North Carolina, the sounds come back to haunt you. The rapid fire of a howitzer battery firing practice rounds at Fort Bragg in the distance echo over the fairway of the golf course. The sound brings with it a flood of memories and suppressed emotions. You feel an uncontrollable urge to run for cover. Why are you standing out in the open? Get down. Where is the whiz? Are the whiz and the boom coming? You have an uncontrollable desire to cry.

But why should a sound you have not heard for over forty years make you cry? The clouds are gone. The sun is shining. The ground is green, not mud. Everything has changed. Only the sound remains the same. The only constants are the sound and your fear of the sound. They remain forever.

CHAPTER FIFTEEN

A Story In Pictures

HIS ALCOHOLIC DAD left him at age two.

As a young child, when his mom was ill, he was placed with cruel foster parents, and was given only one egg to eat for the entire day.

LEFT: Roy as a child in foster care. He was given only one egg to eat for the entire day. For Christmas, even though he and his brother never received any presents, Roy was excited to watch the foster parents' kids open their presents.

RIGHT: Roy Grew up dirt poor. The bat is about the size of his leg. His shoes are too big in order to save on buying shoes when his feet grow bigger.

Roy joined the Marines right out of high school. (*He's second from the right.*)

HOME SWEET HOME: Roy's bed in the barracks. When he slept in foxholes, he used his Zippo lighter to zap the lice out of the seams in his uniform.

[OFFICIAL U.S. MARINE CORPS PHOTO BY PFC SAM BUSHEMI]

LIFE'S BLOOD: His rifle converted into an instrument of mercy to hold the life blood in the bottle. A wounded Marine rests his head on his pack while receiving blood on Okinawa. This was three days before VE day in Europe.

[OFFICIAL U.S. MARINE CORPS PHOTO BY PFC ARTHUR LIAGER]

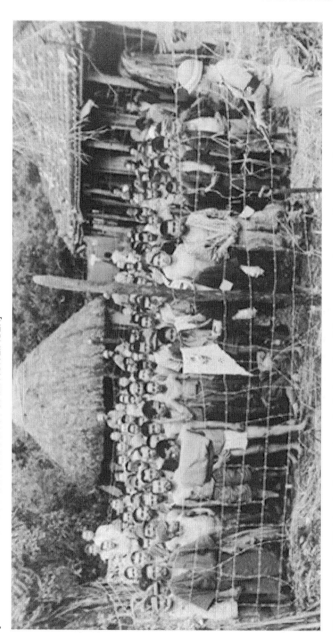

The Sixth Marine Division took an unprecedented number of Japanese as prisoners of war on Okinawa when there, a part of a group of over three hundred, came through the Division's lines to surrender during the final twenty-four hours of battle.

[OFFICIAL U.S. MARINE CORPS PHOTO BY PFC SAM BUSHEMI]

OBSERVING VE DAY: The guns were being silenced in Europe and the capitals of the continent were rejoicing at the end of the war, but on Okinawa a different observance occurred. Jap mortars were pounding the Marine lines. This Marine celebrated the day by having his clothes blown off by a mortar shell. Shocked and hurt, he is helped toward the rear by a companion.

DEATH IN A CREEK: Marines on Okinawa, who met death in a creek from Japanese mortar fire, are removed by their comrades. The bodies of the slain are covered with their ponchos and tenderly hauled up the side of the creek as the journey to the rear begins. [PHOTO CREDIT: U.S. MARINE CORPS PHOTO BY PRIVATE ROBERT BAILEY]

ON THE DOUBLE: Stretcher bearers, bringing in a wounded Marine, run as rapidly as they can with their heavy burden while crossing an open field on Okinawa. Notice the right rear bearer biting his tongue as he labors across the rough ground and the far forward man holding his helmet on his head. [PHOTO CREDIT: OFFICIAL U.S. MARINE CORPS PHOTO BY PFC SAM BUSHEMI]

SEEING THE LIGHT: A Marine rifle man signals his companions to hold their fire as a Japanese soldier emerges from a cave on Okinawa. Persuaded by a smoke grenade, the occupants of the hideout surrendered to the Leathernecks, adding to the large bag of prisoners taken in this Island campaign. [PHOTO CREDIT OFFICIAL U.S. MARINE CORPS PHOTO BY PFC FRANK ROGERS]

BOMB CRATER BATHING: Marines bathe and wash their clothes in a bomb crater located on Naha airfield, which was taken only a few days previous. In the background is the wreckage of a Japanese plane. [PHOTO CREDIT: OFFICIAL U.S. MARINE CORPS PHOTO BY SERGEANT GEORGE TORRIE]

BANZAI CHARGE IN REVERSE: Contrary to the Japanese policy of dying for the Emperor, these Sons of Heaven charge up an Okinawa hillside to surrender after they were flushed from their hiding place by Marine forces. Note the tail-end-Charlie toting the flag of truce. [PHOTO CREDIT: OFFICIAL U.S. MARINE CORPS PHOTO BY PFC JAMES HINDS]

FORWARD AID STATION: While the fighting rages about the enemy's line protecting southern Okinawa, forward aid stations receive the injured Marines and give them immediate treatment. The Corpsmen have strung up a wire to hold the bottles of invaluable blood life plasma. (PHOTO CREDIT: OFFICIAL U.S. MARINE CORPS PHOTO BY SGT. JAMES D. WASDEN)

WOUNDED JAP: Members of a Marine demolitions crew load a wounded Jap prisoner on a stretcher in preparation for evacuation to the nearest medical aid center. The Jap was taken out of a cace by the marines, where he had been hiding to continue his sniper fire. [PHOTO CREDIT: OFFICIAL U.S. MARINE CORPS PHOTO BY CORPORAL JOHN J. CURRAN]

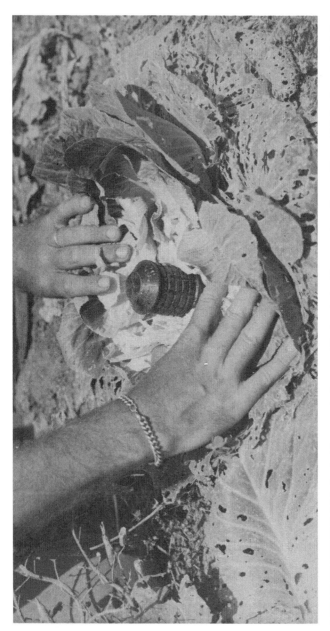

LETHAL VEGETABLE: A Marine holds apart the leaves of the head of cabbage to show the position which the Japanese left the grenade. The enemy cut out the heart of the cabbage and inserted defragmentation hand grenade with the pin pulled. Sharp eye Marine ordnancemen discovered nearly every trick of the Japs before damage was caused on this island in the Ryukyu islands. [PHOTO CREDIT: U.S. MARINE CORPS PHOTO BY LIEUTENANT P.W. SASSEN]

OKINAWA JUNE 1945: TBM dropping two five-hundred pound bombs. [PHOTO CREDIT: U.S. MARINE CORPS PHOTO BY LIEUTENANT DAVID D. DUNCAN]

SNIPER HUNTERS: Marine patrols of the Sixth Division search the ruins in the city of Naha, capital of Okinawa, for Japanese snipers. [PHOTO CREDIT: OFFICIAL U.S. MARINE CORPS PHOTO BY CORPORAL FRANKLIN KERSHAW]

JAP SNIPER: Below Shuri Castle, on Okinawa, a Japanese sniper hides in a Christian church. The Marines in the foreground cover the sniper's lair in the church steeple while a patrol moves in from the rear. [PHOTO CREDIT: OFFICIAL U.S. MARINE CORPS PHOTO BY PRIVATE FIRST CLASS JOHN T. SMITH]

EVACUATION: Stretcher bearers, here, move a Marine casualty to an aid station to the rear without wasting any time. This Marine was wounded during the bloody fighting on Okinawa. [PHOTO CREDIT: OFFICIAL U.S. MARINES CORPS PHOTO BY PRIVATE FIRST CLASS F.R. CHAMBERLAIN]

PINNED DOWN: Temporarily, during their fight among the wrecked homes and rubble of Naha, capital city of Okinawa Island, Sixth Division Marines are pinned down by the fire of Japs. They take cover behind a wall and one peers cautiously around the corner to see what is ahead of them. [PHOTO CREDIT: U.S. MARINE CORPS PHOTO BY PFC JOHN T. SMITH]

INTO THE VALLEY OF DEATH : A stirring photograph that seems to speak the words, "Into the valley of death." [PHOTO CREDIT: OFFICIAL U.S. MARINE CORPS PHOTO BY PRIVATE FIRST CLASS F.R. CHAMBERLAIN]

A CITY LAID WASTE : A Sixth Division Marine stops, high in the hills of Okinawa, to gaze at the ruins of Naha.
[PHOTO CREDIT: OFFICIAL U.S. MARINES CORPS PHOTO BY CORPORAL A.J. GIOSSI]

Roy and the Marines would be on guard duty at this tower.

SURPRISE: When this Marine flame throwing tank discharged a stream of its fire into what was believed to be a Japanese infested cave on Okinawa, a surprise explosion occurred, the place was an enemy ammunition dump. In the foreground First Marine Division men wait for the area to be cleared. [PHOTO CREDIT: OFFICIAL U.S. MARINE CORPS PHOTO BY PRIVATE JOSEPH GUDAS]

Roy became friends with the Japanese and did business with them.

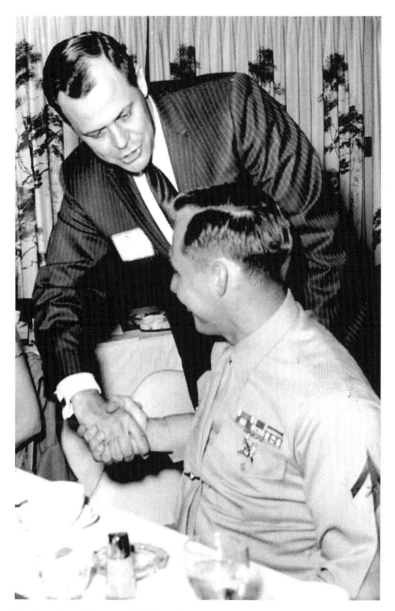

Roy loved meeting people in the military.

"War is the most brutal aspect of human existence. War encompasses all that is evil in the world - death, torture, excruciating pain, rape, dismemberment, and sorrow — in the name of an ideology, government, or religion.

Its scars extend beyond the warfighter to family, friends, and colleagues.

The act of going to war is often decided by those who do not go to fight and, perhaps, never donned a uniform. But for those who do go, the complexities and mistakes made during war can be widespread and last a lifetime."

- Lt. Col. Jaime Parent, USAF, author of Moving Past PTSD

REFLECTIONS

INTERVIEWS

Marine Corps Interview

FROM THE MARINE CORPS ARCHIVES FILMED AT THEIR 2007 REUNION.

INTERVIEWER: PFC Wilkes served in the Marine Corps in World War II for over two and a half years. He was in the 6th Division with the Charlie Company, First Battalion, 29th Marines at Okinawa as a rifleman; that unit was disbanded and after the end of the war he served in the 1st Marine Division in Northern China.

What you were doing before you joined the Marine Corps?

ROY: Right out of high school I joined the Marine Corps because my older brother was in the Marines, so I thought that was the thing to do. He did the thinking. He was smart enough to get in the Marine Air Corps and he didn't tell me there was a big difference between the Marine Air Corps and infantry. I got in the infantry.

INT: Then like a lot of guys, you went to Parris Island . . .

ROY: That's right. And then after Parris Island, you got out of the boot camp and went to Camp Lejeune in North Carolina, which was another tent camp. And then from Camp Lejeune, I went to Camp Pendleton in California. And then from there, I was shipped overseas.

The maybe memorable thing would be at that time it was legal to give IQ tests at boot camp. When they were interviewing me for what branch I should go into, they said, "Gee, you did 149 on your IQ test. How did you do that?"

And I said, "I sat next to a smart guy."

And they said, "OK!"—stamped me for infantry. There were no more questions asked. If I was gonna be a wise guy, I belonged in the infantry. So I went.

But then later on when I was in China, I got a fleet recommendation for Annapolis [United States Naval Academy]. They said, "We've sent a lot of good Marines to Annapolis and they flunked out because of the educational requirements. Now, we decided to send a smart Marine, not necessarily a good Marine. So, we're going to give you a chance." So I got a recommendation for Annapolis.

INT: *At Camp Pendleton, is that where you found out you were in the 29th?*

ROY: No. They would make replacement drafts for replacement battalions to be sent overseas. Once you get overseas, they're divided up as to where the casualties are. Some would go in the first, some in the sixth, and so forth. So I was in the 46th replacement battalion.

INT: *Tell me about your trip to Okinawa. Where did you stop?*

ROY: We stopped at Guam, then went to Okinawa. The thing that was memorable there was when you get to Okinawa, you could look in every direction and see ships. It looked like you could walk across the ocean on ships. There were that many ships there. It was just . . . just amazing how many ships that were there.

INT: *Yeah, I think I've read it was more than D-Day at Normandy. Right?*

ROY: Yes. There were more ships involved than D-Day, but with D-Day they only had to transport stuff like twenty-one miles from England to the coast of France. Here, they had to transport stuff like 10,000 miles, so it was a much bigger job than Normandy.

INT: *So tell me about your experience going in and where did you go first?*

ROY: All the resistance happened at the Naha Shuri Yanabaru Line. We were sent in as replacements at Naha. That was where the fighting had really just begun.

INT: *Did they break you in slowly to combat?*

ROY: No. No. No. [Sigh.] That was unbelievable because all of a sudden we were in this outfit. They broke everybody up. Three went here, four went there, and I kept moving forward. I asked the guy in charge, there were no more lieutenants, there were corporals and sergeants acting. So I asked one of 'em, "Could I load up, you know, put ammunition in my rifle?"

He looked at me and laughed, and said, "C'mere."

We were behind a wall. He said, "Look at that building

"The American "victory" at Okinawa sobered the Allied high command like no other. The largest amphibious armada ever assembled, bigger even than Normandy, had still taken almost three months to subdue the Japanese 32nd Army in the southern half of the island."

- P.T. Deutermann, Award-winning, military author

over there. You see people running around?"

I said, "Yeah."

He said, "Those are Japs. I would suggest you load up."
[Roy laughs.]

So I loaded up. [laughs] Not too bright.

INT: ***When did you first fire a shot and when did you first
get into the thick of it?***

ROY: Well . . . [sigh] we were assigned to guard a bridge right
back in the front, over a small creek. We were there for a
couple days. Then we went back into the front. We had a
lieutenant and we had a company commander then. We
were in back of this wall and we're getting shots from a
Japanese Nambu [pistol]. There was a break in the wall
and the lieutenant called the captain over and said,
"I've located the Nambu. It's right over there." [Roy points
in the distance.]

And with that, there was a burst of fire from the Nambu,
taking a bullet right across the chest for the lieutenant
and the captain. They were both killed instantly.

And then they pulled 'em out and put them on stretchers.
And we were retreating—getting out of there because our
officers had been killed and we were a little screwed up.
So we were pulling back to our other position.

And one of the vivid memories is I looked down and they
were carrying this guy and his arms were straight out [ex-
tends both arms straight out to the sides shoulder level]
and to me it seemed like rigor mortis had already set in
because his arms were bouncing as they were running

with him. And I asked a guy, "Who's that?"
And he said, "It's Lieutenant White."

I couldn't believe how fast his appearance had changed. He just didn't seem the same! His face was gray. So that was my first experience of seeing people killed that fast.

INT: *The Japanese really had some good snipers there. They were really doing a number on all of the battalion commanders — all the spotters. Anybody who had to direct the fire really put their self in harm's way.*

ROY: That's right. They really were efficient at that.
But, for the rest of the war, I tried to stay out of harm's way. I am definitely not a hero. I never did anything heroic. I feel I would be breaking faith with everyone if I tried to make myself out to be some heroic guy. I was frightened.

INT: *Where'd you go on from there?*

ROY: Oh, one of the stories that should be told is . . . I gave you that little piece of information about the Charlie company. We had taken a hill. That morning [Memorial Day, 1945], the sergeant came and he had a lieutenant with him. And he said, "This is our new lieutenant."

[OFFICIAL U.S. MARINE CORPS PHOTO BY PRIVATE FIRST CLASS JOHN T. SMITH]

SHURI CASTLE: Marines of the First Division move warily about the bodies of Japanese who died defending Shuri Castle.

[OFFICIAL U.S. MARINE CORPS PHOTO 120182]

10 May 1945, "VE" PLUS TWO: Two days after the victory in Europe was celebrated the Marines of the First Division, fighting the do-or-die Japs hill by hill in their drive for Naha, capital city of Okinawa, wait on the crest of one slope while a barrage of phosphorous shells explodes among the Japanese positions on the farther incline. After the bombardment, the Leatherneck infantry will commence their push across the intervening valley to attack the enemy.

[DEPARTMENT DEFENSE PHOTO MARINE CORPS, CPL. ARTHUR F. HAGER]

Marine stands in wreckage in theater building in Naha.

We were dug in, and this lieutenant came from hole to hole shaking hands with each private. Well, that was unusual. You didn't shake hands with a lieutenant, so he was very friendly. He shook hands with me. I thought, wow. I never shook hands with a lieutenant before. But he shook hands and smiled.

After he left somebody said he was the captain of the Notre Dame football team. If you look in the records, you'll see that the captain of that team was killed on Okinawa. That was the lieutenant that came up that day to help us or to lead us.

But talk about pressure. Here's a guy who's joining a group of men who have been on the front lines for a long time. Many of them had already been killed. And now he's joining them and is supposed to lead them. Pressure-packed job coming in, right into a combat situation.

We knew that after we took this hill the Japanese would fall back to another line of defense. Well, we wouldn't know whether that line of defense was fifty yards back, or a hundred yards back, or one hundred fifty. You wouldn't know where the hell it was. There was still vegetation in this area, so the Japanese had natural camouflage and concealment.

So they sent a platoon to find out where the next line of defense was. Well, that's a bad, that's a bad assignment because you're out there to draw fire [and respond with artillery].

And thank God I'm way in the back. We went out single file. And I'd say . . . well, I know there were twenty-five of us.

And the lieutenant, I think because he was new, wanted to lead everyone. So it was, "Follow me, men."
And he was up at the point. In the article there, it says he threw a grenade into a tomb. It wasn't a tomb. It was a cave. And it was a long cave filled with explosives. When he threw the grenade, this whole hillside went up—I mean, like, ten stories high. I can't tell you how much dirt and rocks were thrown in the air. So much that the first twenty-two men were completely covered—buried alive.

There was so much dust and dirt in the air. No one could see what the hell was in there. I was covered from my neck down, chest out, arms covered. And my good friend *[and another Marine were]* also covered. We were the last three in the column.

And then the Japs started throwing shelling in that area to make sure that everybody was killed. So with the shelling, it was a dangerous place to be.

[Our guys] were watching us with glasses from [a position in] the back. So they get three volunteers, to come in and see if anybody is still alive in that mess. One of 'em was a corpsman and [two others] were carrying one stretcher.

And so they came in and started digging me out and I said I was all right. I asked 'em to take care of Bobbie, who was my good friend. They started digging Bobbie out and tried to find out what the hell was wrong with him. He was turning gray and found out that he had been shot.

We shouldn't have been that close together [when we went in]. He was alongside of me. I had loaded and my safety was off because we were in front of the lines. We expected a firefight.

When the explosion came, I fell forward and shot Bobbie, and he was blown six feet in front of me and he died. And then the fellow in back of me was unconscious, but I think he lived.

They put the one guy on a stretcher, and they couldn't believe that I could walk. I said, "Yeah, I can walk."

Out of the twenty-five people, there were twenty-three that were dead now . . . the first twenty-two [who] were buried, [plus] Bobbie. So they said we were going to go back, [to] carry [the unconscious Marine] back. And [they said,] You run alongside of us.

I got out. But that was the . . . That was when I lost all my friends there. The whole unit was wiped out.

INT: **Wow. So when he threw the grenade in there, he hit an ammo dump.**

ROY: Yes. There's so much talk and scuttlebutt. The next day they were saying—I heard that there was, and I'd never even bothered to look this up—that there was picric acid *[a component of military explosives]* . . . I don't even know what picric acid is, but they said that's why the whole thing blew up so fast. But anyway, it was a hell of an explosion.

INT: *Was that it for you, then?*

ROY: No, no, oh, no.

INT: *You came back?*

ROY: In fact, they sent me to battalion aid. Even though I could walk, they said, "No, you can't, you got to go back to battalion first aid." So I went back to battalion first aid. I had got bonked on the head, because my helmet came off. And had to have my head wrapped up.

I walked back [to first aid]. And they put a big tag on you. Saying what's wrong. And this gives the corpsman back at battalion aid a roadmap as to who to see next. Well, shit, there were so many guys who were being seriously hurt that were coming back, I just sat there for a couple of hours. And I sat there and begin to feel guilty that all these guys were hurt and I wasn't.

I went back to my outfit and told them that I took the tag off myself. I said that I'm okay.

INT: *Is that how you got the Purple Heart?*

ROY: Yeah. You know, that was a funny thing. I was so afraid that back at battalion aid they were gonna send my mother

Medals Roy Wilkes received.

this telegram — you know, your son has been wounded in action — so I said, "Well, I'm not wounded! I'm not wounded! I'm not wounded, don't send my mother any telegram." And I'm talking about sending my mother a telegram, and asking them not to do that, and they're rollin' their eyes. They don't know who's gonna get a telegram and who isn't going to. So, I thought that I wouldn't get any Purple Heart or anything because I kept telling them, "I'm not wounded and I'm all right. And look, I'm going back to my outfit."

I was just away from my outfit for, you know, a night.

But when I was in China, they said the following men are going to get Purple Hearts for wounds in Okinawa. And I was one of them. I couldn't believe it. I got the Purple Heart late when I was in China, but it was for Okinawa.

And my mother never did get a telegram.

INT: *Yeah, you don't want that to happen. No.*

ROY: No.

INT: *So, what'd you do after that? You're back, just . . . When was that? In May?*

ROY: Probably . . . Yeah, that was in May [1945].

Then one other story about Okinawa . . . on a place called Love Hill. Well, once again, it was one of those things where the Marines had gone in and taken the hill and then got the hell shot out of 'em. They were falling back, carrying their dead and wounded. And we made an advance through their retreat to get up on the hill. So we got up on the hill. There were maybe ten, twelve of us.

That night on Love Hill, three of the twelve got Silver Stars, which is unusual, you know, for three men out of twelve to get Silver Stars. *[The Silver Star Medal is the United States Armed Forces' third-highest personal decoration for valor in combat. The Silver Star is awarded primarily to members of United States Armed Forces for gallantry in action against an enemy of United States.]*

My good friend Todd received the Silver Star. He was an older guy, and he had a wife and kids. And we were dug in. He was on the left flank. I was on the right flank. And the lieutenant and the sergeant were in the center.

Well, they started coming up on the sides of the hill, you know. And Todd stood up, and he had a BAR [Browning Automatic Rifle]. A bullet hit the stock of the BAR. It broke the stock. *[A stock is the part of a rifle to which the barrel and firing mechanism is attached. It's held firmly against the shooter's shoulder when firing the gun.]* He's firing this BAR with no stock on it!

But . . . and he was wounded. He had every right to get off that hill, to go back. He refused. Until the next morning when they saw how much blood he lost. Then they finally told him that they had to get him off there.

There was also a replacement who just came up that day.

And when we got up on the hill, the replacement decided that we couldn't hold the hill and he took off and went back. A year later they were still court-martialing that guy in China for taking off.

That shows the contrast there. Todd, who got the Silver Star. And I don't blame the kid who ran back. But that shows a contrast in people.

And then on my side, there were three of us on the right side of the hill. Once again, another replacement — well, two replacements. One on my left was a kid and the guy on my right was a former Raider! [Marine Raiders are an elite special operations force of the USMC]. You have to respect the Raiders. They were throwing grenades in. And, uh . . . [sigh] to make a long story short [sigh, pause], [the Raider] said, "If another grenade comes in, I'll take care of it."

And just as he said that, another grenade came in. We got down. He grabbed his rifle and charged up the hill. It was about twenty yards to the top of it, to the crest of the hill. And then they were on the other side, and we were on this side. We were exchanging grenades. They had a knee boarder there [a Japanese soldier with a clipboard strapped to one leg], [and] . . . they were shooting up at us also.

So [the Raider] ran up to do what he can, to take care of the . . . and he threw some grenades and got shot too. There was a sniper on the right. And when we got there, the Marines who had retreated had left a dead Marine there. They did everything they could to take all their own wounded and dead back. But this guy they couldn't carry because everybody was carrying somebody. So they left this dead Marine there.

And it showed me the proficiency of the sniper over here. So I just kept my head down—diggin' like hell. In a short time, I had a pretty deep hole. I could have dug my way out, all the way to America if I had given it another couple of hours.

Anyway, [the Raider] charged up and he got the Silver Star. This Japanese sniper fired one shot that went through both of his knees while he's running. How do your knees have to be for one shot to go through both of 'em? But anyway, he rolled down and they took him back.

Then the third guy [who] got the Silver Star was the corpsman in the center because he kept taking wounded back. And as he'd come back, he'd keep bringing grenades and ammunition back. But we were, I don't know, at least 300 yards in front of the lines. So that area in between there was occupied by the Japs because they were tryin' to take the hill from all directions. [The corpsman would] actually be going through their area, coming back and forth. He didn't get wounded, but he did get the Silver Star.

We held that hill that night, and in the morning, the rest of the guys came. And there was no firing, there was no . . . You know, they were all walking around . . . But that's the way things would work out, where you'd be in a tremendous battle, and then a few minutes later, why, that's over and you're just up and walking around and nobody's there.

INT: *So, after Okinawa you want to go to Guam?*

ROY: Well, one other thing on Okinawa. There was a small island off of Naha. We could walk to that island when the tide was out. But when the tide came in, it was an island. They decided to locate in the morning—the tide is out. We're gonna walk to that island and take that island because we had to take that out before we could take Oroku Peninsula, which was another landing.

So anyway, I was the second man. I was a runner at the time. The captain was gung-ho and you had to be with him. He was leading a group and we took the island. There was practically nobody on it. Thank God. If there had been anyone on it, we would have been toast. Anyway, we took that little island.

Then we came back and the next day we go to the landing on the Oroku Peninsula.

INT: *That was a last-minute plan?*

ROY: It was a last-minute plan, right. The way they decided was that they had all these amtracs [amphibious, tracked troop & supply support vehicles], and they pull all these amtracs along the sea wall. *[A sea wall is a man-made barrier designed to contain a large body of water (as in a flood-prone area); in wartime, a sea wall can be a defensive construction designed to hinder water-borne operations of the enemy.]*

We got on the amtrac from the sea wall and that was near Naha. And then they pull straight out, and now the Oroku Peninsula is over here [points in the distance]. While we were going out, it was the most amazing thing because they had several battleships anchored out there. And they were firing full blast at this Oroku Peninsula. And then on top of that, they had all these cruisers and destroyers—all of 'em were firing. So, you'd hear the blast from the guns, and then the shells whistling overhead, and then the explosion. That in itself was deafening, but we went underneath all of that, while they were doing that.

While we're going in a straight line . . . the Japs were trying to put mortars into the landing craft, so there'd be an explosion here and the explosion there.

Then all of a sudden, the firing stopped . . . and there was an air strike. And boy, when the planes come in to make an airstrike—they're noisy. Plane after plane would come in straight to the beach, in front of us.

And then all of a sudden the air strike stopped. Now, it was such a contrast because the firing had stopped . . . we also had our own Marine artillery. All the artillery stopped, the airstrikes stopped. And then all the ships, the amtracs just turned and head toward the beach. Well, that gets your attention.

Now I know this sounds crazy. Maybe it's bad planning, but the amtracs turn to go towards shore. And one of the guys next to me says, "Hey, how the hell do we get out of this thing?"

And I looked and thought, that's right, this amtrac is being driven in the front, and there's no ramp in the front. Every landing craft we had been in up to that time had a ramp in the front, and it was driven by a sailor, in the back. This one had a Marine in the front driving the thing, and there's a .50-caliber machine gun up there and an officer, but no ramp in the front.

So, there are three people in the front of the landing craft. We're all down in the craft. We're wondering how the hell we get out of this thing because there's no ramp. And you start lookin' around and one of the guys says, "There's a ramp in the back!"

You know, the amtrac goes into the water then the tracks bring it up on the beach. It can go pretty far on the beach, as far as you want it to go. Then the ramp in the back falls down and you get out.

But the lieutenant up [at] the front said, "You will go over the side."

Well, shit, the thing is, I don't know, six, seven, eight feet high seems high. One of the guys said, "Oh, no, that'd be too dangerous! You don't wanna climb over the side unless you're a target; we'll go out the back."

The lieutenant said, "The orders are, you are going over the side!" And that put an end to the discussion.

But that showed Marine Corps discipline also. Okay, to get on the beach, we're going to go over the side of this thing.

And I don't know why, but . . . we went over the side, and got up on the beach.

We landed on this Oroku Peninsula and we were supposed to be there. The Japanese are supposed to realize, oh, we're in back of them now. The whole Shuri Naha Yonabaru Line was supposed to collapse because the Marines have landed in back of 'em.

Well, they found out that this Oroku Peninsula was fortified better than Corregidor. *(More than 6,000 Japanese troops had been on Corregidor in February 1945—far more than the U.S. military had estimated.)*

All they allowed us to do is get on the beach. We get maybe a couple hundred yards in and we meet a lot of resistance. So we can't move. We're pinned down. And they're gonna move another, and another part, and we're going to just hold our ground here.

So, it's getting late in the day and we're pinned down there. And I decide, well, I'm going to walk back to the beachhead and see if there's anything there for us.

What the Marines do is you make a midnight requisition

of things that you need, in other words—you steal. So I decided to go out on a requisition.

I walk back to the beachhead, and . . . now, this shows you also the mentality of the Marines. You're unloading stuff for the beachhead. You've already got Marine Corps guards guarding that, not from the Japanese, *but from the Marines*—so we don't steal it!

So, look, I think, okay, so you've got maybe a pile of goods there that are a couple hundred yards long, and maybe a hundred yards wide. And they've got Marines walking around that, making sure that nobody gets in there and steals anything.

I see that. I get up there and I start walking around it too, carrying my rifle — like I'm guarding it. And all of a sudden I bumped into the guard on the other side and he says, "Hey, what the hell you doin' here?"
I said, "This is my post."
He says, "Oh, no."
I said, "Yeah, yeah, your post head is over there."
He says, "Well, okay."

So now he thinks his post ends about fifty yards down. Now I got this whole area that I can survey and see what I can steal.

So I run and look and see what the hell is available. And I see there was a plastic carton and it had a chicken in it! A whole chicken. I couldn't believe that, that there's a chicken there! What the hell is a chicken doin' here on top of everything? So . . . I grabbed the chicken and the only other thing I could find real quick was like a five-gallon can of peaches. And I grab the five-gallon can of peaches and took off.

I took that to where we were on the lines. I said, "Hey look, I got a chicken." We take the chicken and we cut it up in fourteen pieces and we bake it over a little can of Sterno [canned heat]. Each guy has a little piece of chicken that he puts on his Ka-Bar [combat] knife and bakes it over his can of Sterno. We had fourteen guys eating chicken. Then somebody comes up to me and says, "You know, we should really give the lieutenant and the sergeant pieces." I say, "You're very smart."

I go up to the lieutenant, "Would you like a piece of chicken?"

"Where'd you get the chicken?"

I said, "Oh, it was a Gook chicken." "Gook" means anything on the island is gook. In other words, the natives owned it. He didn't bother to ask me, was it dressed or how come it's raw? Fine. He eats his chicken. And the sergeant eats his chicken.

Then the colonel called a meeting and all the company commanders went back to this meeting. And when he came back he said, "Boy, was the colonel pissed off."

"Why?"

He said he knew a chef on one of those ships. And the chef sent him a chicken. And would you believe it? Somebody stole that chicken off the beachhead. They stole the colonel's chicken!"

[Gasps.] I said, "That's terrible! Oh, goodness gracious."

[Laughs.]
That was my chicken story.

INT: *He didn't rat you out?*

ROY: Oh, no. No.

INT: *Did you go on to the southern tip [of Okinawa] and then do a mopping up there?*

ROY: Yes, the southern tip . . . we went to the southern tip. [sighs] A lot of things happened in the southern tip . . . there were so many bodies. Anybody that's been really on frontline duty at Okinawa has to be amazed at the number of unburied dead. If you read about Okinawa it says 250,000 Okinawans and Japanese lost their lives. Well, I'd say of the 250,000, probably 200,000 plus more than that were unburied. So, it would rain on 'em and they would get bloated. When the rain stopped and the sun came out—after you're dead, you still continue to get tan because it seems they'd get burned and black. And then the maggots and flies would come. But that would be . . . as far as you could see—there'd be bodies! That was, uh . . . life became very cheap. Life became very cheap on the southern tip. But at least the most of the fighting was over. And we had little . . .

I just thought of one more story. Well, yesterday at the reunion, these new Marines were showing us this sophisticated stuff that they now have. And they demonstrated these advanced sound things where they could tell if there's any movement out there. Motion detectors. That was the latest thing, their motion detectors.

And I said, "Shit, we had those fifty years ago."

They questioned, "You had motion detectors fifty years ago?"

I said, "Yeah."

What are you talking about?"

Okay, at the southern tip we were flushing [Japanese soldiers from] caves. That was the day job. Then at night, we'd all pull back and we had a big circle. There was this concertina barbed wire all around us, so that would be protecting us. And we had tents in that circle. And then guards [were posted] because the Japs would come out of the caves and want to get food and so forth. It was like the Wild West. We were living inside the circle with the barbed wire, concertina barbed wire all around us.

The smart Marines decided, well, what the hell, somebody can come in [through] that wire.

So with the C-Rations, we'd get a can of something or other. They'd take their Ka-Bar [combat]] knife and jab a hole in the bottom of the can. And then take a string of barbed wire and put it through so that the wire could go all the way through. And then take that wire and just hang it on the other barbed wire, then they'd hang another can right next to it. And another can right next to it.

So now you look and you see this barbed wire protecting us, but it's got all these tin cans hanging on it. But if you're near that barbed wire and touch it — *dingalinglingling* — all these cans bump against each other. It would make a hell of a racket!

So we invented the motion sound detector. [laughs] It was a little cruder than what they have now, but that's what we'd use. So sometimes a rat or something would jingle the wire and everybody would get excited, but the Japs really never tried to come in. They just wanted to go someplace other than the southern tip.

INT: *We're going to talk about China here. And some of these photographs you gave me. After Okinawa, you went to Guam?*

ROY: That's right, after Okinawa we went to Guam and we thought we're going to go home now because America is going to reward its Marine Corps for these battles!

We're watching a movie one night and they said, "Report to your barracks." We reported to our barracks, and we heard, "Pack up, pack up your sea bags, we're moving out tonight."

"Wow." We thought, boy oh boy, thank God for America! You know, America can't do too much for their Marines. America wants to really help their Marine Corps get home, you know it! We're goin' home! Wow, is this great! We're the first ones to go home, and look how fast they want us to go home, too!

Then the ship took off and we thought, we don't like the looks of this, because there's so damn many ships. I mean, there are a lot of ships here. And then all of a sudden we see aircraft carriers in the distance. Say, what the hell?

Are they escorting us back? Or what?

Then finally, one of the smarter guys said, "Hey, you guys think you're going home?"

"Huh? Yeah. Where else can we be going?"

"Well, you're going northwest because the sun's coming up there and it should be coming up there, and we're going northwest."

"What the hell is northwest?"

"China is west. China is also northwest."

After a couple of days . . . and then there was a bigger armada there. We see land. It's not San Francisco. We see land, and we hear, "You're going to make a simulated battle landing at Tsingtao, China." *[Tsingtao is a coastal city on the Yellow Sea.]*

One of the guy says, "I hope I don't get hit with a simulated bullet!"

So anyway, we make the simulated battle landing, and the Chinese are there yellin' and they're happy because that means that the Japanese are going to go and they hated the Japs. And they thought we were going to be friendly. Japs had been very hard on them.

So we hit the beach, then get put on trucks and get driven through the city.

We were there for, I don't know. There was a big surrender ceremony. What a farce!

They have the Japs lay down their swords on the table. We're all standing there, shit, we had to stand there for about six hours waiting for this to happen. So they hand in all their swords. Then we go back to the barracks. And then they turn around and give all the swords back to 'em—their weapons *back* to 'em.

But the publicity was that we were there to repatriate the Japanese, to take up the Japanese arms and send them back to Japan. That was not what we were there for. We were there to help the Chinese Nationalists. And we didn't take Japanese weapons. Japanese continued to have them. And some of the pictures I gave you showed that.

INT: How long were you in Tsingtao before you were moved up to the Manchurian border?

ROY: I would say a week, week and a half, maybe two weeks. It was nice duty in the city. It was good. And then we were put on ships again and moved up to a place called Ching Wang Tao. It was on the Manchurian border, and—

INT: That was also a prison camp location I think?

ROY: I'm not familiar with the prison camp. Believe it or not, there were French Foreign Legion stationed there, and we relieved them. And then there was a Japanese tuberculosis hospital a little south of there.

INT: Oh, that's right. That was just a port. That was just the location where some of the North China Marines would go and use their rifle range.

ROY: Yeah. Well, shit, wherever the Marines were, there was

a rifle range.

INT: **Then how did you get up to the Manchurian border?**

ROY: Well, they get us on ships. We went up there and then get off at Ching Wang Tao. Then they decided — well, we've gotta keep this railroad open. If this railroad is closed . . . the Communists are in Manchuria. They're comin' down in China. If they take over this railroad, they close the railroad, then all of northern China is gonna freeze to death because all the coal mines were up there, and the one railroad was used to supply coal to all of China.

They said the most important thing is we keep the bridges open. They assigned the Marines to every other bridge. And every other bridge — there weren't enough Marines to guard all the bridges, every other bridge was guarded by the Japanese.

I would say, weeks after the war was over, and weeks after the charade of the Japanese surrendering in Tsingtao, we were guarding bridges with them. The Japanese were fully armed, guarding their bridge. And we depended on them to keep their bridge open. They depended on us to keep our bridge open.

INT: **Did Japan have an interest in that? Did they get some of that coal?**

ROY: No. The interest for the Japanese—after the war was over, all the Japanese wanted to do was go home. I read that if a country surrenders, it's illegal to press their troops into service, but the Japanese were in service helping the Marines and helping the Nationalists. But their only interest was not to help anybody, but to get the hell out of there and go home. And they wanted to do anything that they had to do in order to go home.

INT: ***But you found that some of these guys just kept there doing their job, and they took—***

ROY: Oh, sure.

INT: ***They took orders from American officers?***

ROY: That's right. They took orders from America as to what to do and where to go and what to guard. And they did a good job of it. They were good soldiers.

INT: ***Some of them may have been young and maybe their enlistment was not up and so on.***

ROY: Well, no. I'm talking about the Japanese. They were older. They weren't that young. The Chinese were the young ones. When we bring the Chinese up from South China to the border, and they were the ones who were supposed to relieve us, they would sit down with the Communists and compare and say,
"How long has it been since you've been paid?"
"Oh, we haven't been paid for two years."
"Well, we were paid six months ago. How long are you in for?"
"We're in for life."
"Oh, no, we're in for five years."
"See, you got a better deal."

It was not a great philosophical or political debate. It was—I think I'm going to get more if I'm a Communist than a Nationalist [so] I'm a Communist.

At least that's the way we heard it when we were there.

INT: *Let's go through these photographs. There's just one barracks.*

ROY: All right. That was an isolated barracks that was alongside of this Bridge 54. Fifty of us were assigned Bridge 54. We got off the train and looked at that thing. And then you could see, if you look far enough in one direction you could see the Great China Wall going through the hills. But in every other direction there was desolation. We were to guard that bridge.

They said—well, there's no electricity, no running water, no heat, no light, no telephone, no nothing, but you're only going to be here for a couple of weeks. Make the best of it.

And that night when I got in bed, I looked up, and I could see snow coming through the slots in the roof. So, make the best of it—we were there for nine months. The fifty of us.

Roy stayed in these barracks with no electricity, no running water, no heat, no light, and no telephone. In every other direction there was desolation.

INT: **Just the one bridge.**

ROY: Just the one bridge. Yeah. Well, that was our assignment. At night, we could hear 'em working on the tracks. Everybody knew the ground rules. They wouldn't come near the bridge. We wouldn't shoot them if they were on the tracks.

At night, we could hear 'em working on the tracks. So, a hundred yards away from us, the Chinese wouldy'd tear up all the tracks and carry all those ties away. There'd be no train coming through. They could heat their home for a month with one tie.

Then they made the offense punishable by death. If you got caught with a railroad tie in your home. So the Chinese would take them off in the field and remember where they buried them. You know, the Chinese can wait fifty years. They buried the tracks and that was their 401(k) plan I guess.

INT: **Buried treasure.**

ROY: Yeah.

INT: **Tell me. How many Marines were there at Bridge 54?**

ROY: About fifty of us.

INT: **And did they replace any? Or is it just your group?**

ROY: No. That was just our group. When we came there, it was an empty barracks. And there obviously had been . . . I don't know if there were Chinese or Japanese there prior to us, but when we got there it was an empty barracks.

INT: *And there was no town? You don't have a town name or anything like that?*

ROY: No. Down the tracks, maybe ten miles down, there was a mud village. And in that mud village—the two incentives for visiting the mud village—was that they had a couple of whorehouses and a photography studio.

INT: *Tell me about this photograph with the row of Japanese in the front and the Marines in the back, and everyone's got different uniforms on.*

ROY: All right. That was interesting because a lot of people say—well, we picked up the Japanese weapons; the Japanese weren't armed; we were sending Japanese home. That was taken Christmas of 1945. And the Japanese who had a bridge five miles down put on their dress uniforms, marched down the tracks, five miles. And they came to us, they said—we know this is a special holiday for the Americans; we want to wish you Merry Christmas. And they said, we have only one thing that is of value to us, and that's this German Shepherd dog. We'd like to give you this nice big German Shepherd dog. We'd like to leave him here with you.

So they gave us their dog. We had our picture taken with them. We didn't offer them any beer or any . . . We just said, "Okay, fine, thank you." And then [the Japanese] went and walked back down the tracks to their bridge.

INT: *Did they know why they gave you the dog?*

ROY: That was a sincere . . . They wanted to wish us Merry Christmas. The Chinese didn't wish us Merry Christmas.

INT: *[The dog] wasn't to eat? Right?*

ROY: No, no, it wasn't to eat. It was a pet. And the dog was a great dog. For some reason, he became my dog and he would sleep underneath my cot.

INT: *This other picture is proof positive that...*

ROY: The Japanese were armed. And you could see it's cold there. The Japanese were doing duty with the Marines.

INT: *Now, was there somebody assigned to them from the American troops?*

ROY: No. They were strictly on their own.

INT: *What kept them from deserting do you think?*

ROY: Japanese discipline.

INT: *Tell me about the carload of Chinese. Why were these people being brought out of the area?*

ROY: The train was available and they would get on.

Roy with the dog the Japanese gave to the Marines to sincerely wish them Merry Christmas, 1945. The dog became Roy's pet and slept underneath his cot. Note how sad Roy's eyes look.

In Europe, you know, it was said it was always terrible that the people were riding in these boxcars. Well, here, you could see these are open cars. And the people would get on. And the Marines were there. We were there to load the cars and make sure they didn't carry anything with them. You know, they can't take their furniture or suitcase or anything. They were just to get on the cars and that's it. Leave the things. They leave their pets behind, you know. But . . .

There was tremendous fear of revolution. Now, I don't know whether to call it a China Revolution or China civil war. But the Nationalists were fighting the Communists.

INT: **In Manchuria?**

ROY: In northern China.

And they knew that the Communists had been armed by the Russians in Manchuria, taking the Japanese weapons. And we're arming the Nationalists, eventually we give them Japanese weapons. But the Japs still had their weapons. But they were brought up and they had American weapons.

INT: **This was going to be the point of clash.**

ROY: That's what this was, the point of clash.

What that picture shows is that the Chinese wanted to get out of the way. They didn't want to be Nationalists. They didn't want to be Communists. They wanted to be

PROOF JAPANESE HAD WEAPONS. After the war, the Japanese were on duty with the Marines. *(Roy is third from the left on the second row.)*

live Chinese, so we were loading them on.

Now there's a second picture of me standing there many months later, without the heavy jacket on. Look at how dirty my jacket was and how my hair had grown.

And once again there would be talk about other battles and the Chinese would be getting onto cars, trying to get out of the way again.

INT: *So they came back and they left, and they came back and they left.*

ROY: That's right. They'd come back and leave, and come back and leave.

"The Chinese wanted to get out of the way. They didn't want to be Nationalists. They didn't want to be Communists. They wanted to be live Chinese, so we were loading them on."

Six months later than previous picture. Note the change in Roy.

INT: *Let's talk about the mud village. There was a photo studio and a whorehouse and that was it.*

ROY: Yeah. You took your choice.

INT: *Not even a place to drink. Not . . .*

ROY: No. Not one bar, not one restaurant. Not one car.

INT: *And this was a coal—*

ROY: Coal mining village.

INT: *Who was it built by?*

ROY: It was built originally by the British. And run by the British. And then it was run by the Japanese. Because this area was vital to China. Whoever controlled this area, controlled China. Because this area exported coal for all of the rest of China.

INT: *That's why the Japanese took it.*

ROY: Right. That's why the Japanese took it.

INT: *Took Manchuria.*

ROY: And that's why the Communists wanted it.

INT: *So you and your buddies would go down to the photo studio. In this photo you have your winter gear on.*

ROY: Yeah.

INT: *What time frame is this?*

ROY: Well, this is November, December, January, February, and the weather was—

INT: *Of what year?*

ROY: Of '45 [and into '46]. But the interesting thing is that in order to get into town . . . You see how these trains were loaded. Every train that came by was loaded like that. Well, we would stop a train. And then we'd get on the engine car, the engine coal car. But it was loaded with Chinese at the back. We make it go ten miles down the track and the [Marines] would get off to go to the whorehouse, to get their picture taken, but they'd always leave a couple of guys guarding the engineer. Because if that train left, we'd have a ten-mile walk back to our place. So we didn't want the train to leave. So the train would stay there for a couple hours.

Then the guys would come back, and we tell the train "Back up" and everybody on that train, hundreds, maybe a thousand people, would moan and groan and yell. Because we were going to go back. And they knew that—oh, those Marines are savages. So the train would back up and let us off. Those Marines just went into town for a piece of ass, [the Chinese thought,] and look how we have to suffer. You know. Screw them. [laughs]

INT: *They're very passive . . . pacifist.*

ROY: The thing that the Chinese say—"ting hau, ting hau"—and hold their thumb up. You know. So then we learned—and they'd smile at you—they learned to smile and say "boo-hau, boo-hau" and they thought they were very funny, they were entertaining each other. Because "ting hau" means very good. With the thumb down, "boo-hau" means very bad.

So, they'd be looking at us like, "boo-hau, boo-hau." So finally we learned. No, no, they're saying "very bad."

INT: *The Chinese though, what I'm getting at, is they're very laid back, and I guess, they really take it as it comes.*

ROY: That's right.

INT: *They could have jumped off that train and said, You guys get off of here.*

ROY: No they wouldn't. Because we were all armed and they weren't. It was just Marines being bullies. But after you're there for so long . . .

Another story about the Chinese is we bought a cow one time. Our number one boy—which is a guy about probably seventy years old—went into the town, bought the cow, and brought this cow back, and we killed the cow. And our guy Todd was a butcher, and he hung the cow up under the bridge, skinned him, and oh, boy, we had beef.

So a couple months later he was—let's buy another cow.

Only this time, instead, the whole village walked over to see the negotiation, they brought the cow, and opened the wire, and they brought the cow inside the wire—"How much?"

And the price had gone up like a thousand percent. And they're laughing, and they thought that was just great— hahaha.

INT: *They liked to haggle.*

ROY: Yeah. Well, they haggle. Also, they were screwin' the Marines.

Then we realized, okay, they're really not coming down in the price.
This one Marine went out there . . . He took out a .45 and—pow—shot the cow in the head. The cow fell right down.
[The Marine] said, "The cow is trespassing; you know nothing is supposed to come through the wire. Get the cow out of here!"

And everybody else outside went—oooh—because that was bad. Number one boy looked, and he started crying, he said, "Oh, please, please buy the cow now."

He said, "No, we don't want the cow. Get him outta here!"

That whole village was so quiet, it was unbelievable. This cow was bleeding; they pulled him out by his back leg. Open up the wire, pull the cow out, shut the wire.

So, I wonder why the Marines' relationship with the Chinese was a little stressed? I can't figure it out.

INT: *[laughs] And they didn't come in and demand a crazy price again, did they?*

ROY: Oh, no. There were no more negotiations. After the Marines shot the cow . . . and those poor people had to pull that cow back like five miles by the legs. They're pulling. They didn't want to start skinning it right there and have us see. The whole village is taking turns pulling that cow back. Because they didn't want a dead cow. They weren't going to eat it.

INT: *That village was hoping to make money for probably everybody in the village.*

ROY: That's right. They wanted to take advantage of the Marines. And then after that, really, we had sub-posts off the bridge, down the tracks a bit after a while. And those isolated posts, there was a Marine killed because farmers came and started talkin' to the guy and while they were talking to the guy, another farmer snuck up in back and hit him with a hoe right in the back of the neck. And took his rifle.

INT: *I have five minutes left. Tell me quickly. All these different people posed with you guys at the photo studio.*

ROY: Yeah. There were the Chinese militia there. They were the people on the right. People on the left are the Chinese Nationalists. Guys in the front are the Marines. And in addition to that, there were the Japanese. There were four armed groups in town—the Nationalists, the militia, the Japs, the Marines, and then occasionally the Communists would get in there.

If you went into town, you had to bring a piece. You had to bring over a rifle or a pistol with you.

Posing at photography studio. Roy is at the far right.

Marines posing with Chinese militia and Japanese soldiers. [ROY NOT IN PHOTO]

INT: *And what's unique about this is that you guys didn't just bring this for a photo shoot. These are the weapons that you carried with you at all times.*

ROY: Right. To get into town.

INT: *And there is a reason that you got together for the photo? Or was—*

ROY: Well, everybody was mingling around in the street. And some guys were having their picture taken, and the studio was, hey, let's all get together. Hey you, come here. You, come here, get in here.

So we all got together and said, "Okay, there's our shoot."

INT: *I'll sum it up then. I've got about four minutes, and I just want to wrap it up.*

How long were you in China altogether?

ROY: A little less than a year, I'd say around a year.

INT: *You got out about, mid '46.*

ROY: I think. Yeah, it was mid '46. Yeah. Had to be.

INT: *And where did you go from there?*

ROY: I came home and I was home for about a week and then I went to college.

Thank God for the Marine Corps because I was able to go to college. And if it weren't for the Marines, I would have never gone to school.

INT: *What degree did you get? And just tell me, where did you retire from, and all that?*

ROY: Well, I eventually got a degree from St Mary's College in Winona, Minnesota. And then went out and got a job like everybody else. And eventually I formed my own company. And I still work. I'm an old man but I'm still working. Because I'm president. [Roy started the company, Wilkes and McLean, that still sells hydraulic noise suppressors and accumulators.] I don't do any heavy lifting. But I have the company and it's been a wonderful experience.

INT: *Looking back over your life, is there some way you could sum up how being a Marine has changed your life? Anything?*

ROY: Oh, it sure has. First, I truly feel that I wasn't a good Marine. And I'm not being humble. I saw good Marines, so I know what a good Marine is.

I was a teen and I was scared shitless. I was really frightened when I was in combat. But I had a front row seat. I saw more combat than most guys. It just happened that way that I had a chance to see it. But I saw heroes. I saw good Marines. And I'm not one of 'em.

But by golly, the Marine Corps has changed my life. Because as I got older, I had a deeper appreciation of the

Corps, and the values that they inculcate into you. And coming here today, this weekend, and hearing some of the talks, I go—yeah, they're right when they talk about duty and honor and all of that.

And as you get older, it means more. That's what I owe to the Marine Corps. I'm proud. I'm more proud today to be a Marine than I was when I was eighteen years old.

INT: ***OK. Thanks, Roy.***

ROY: Thanks.

REFLECTIONS II

DOCUMENTARY
INTERVIEW

FROM BOB ZIMMERMAN'S (2015) WORLD WAR II DOCUMENTARY, *RISE OF THE VALIANT*

INTERVIEWER: When you went overseas, where did you go first?

ROY: Overseas we first went to Guam, and that was the staging area for going to Okinawa. We were not in the original Marines that landed on Okinawa. We were a replacement battalion. We didn't get there until the battle was a couple of weeks old. That's when we joined them.

INT: You didn't make the original landing?

ROY: No, did not make the original—

INT: About two weeks later.

ROY: Right. Then the 6th Marine Division went north when they landed on Okinawa. And by the time I got there, we were pretty much finished up north and we all thought we were going to go home. We were just delighted that, hey, this was a cakewalk for us!

Then they told us, "No, the army has run into a lot of resistance at the southern tip." That's where all the fighting in Okinawa took place, on the southern tip of the island. The Japs gave the Marines practically ninety percent of the island, with very little resistance—very little fighting. But that last, the southern tip of Okinawa is where all the casualties took place with a lot of the fighting. That's when I joined the 6th Division and we went south.

INT: *Once everybody went north, probably in May when things really started . . .*

ROY: Latter part of April I'd say. Then they pulled the old bit where they pull an army division out of the lines and put a Marine Corps division in there, because the Army wasn't keeping pace with the Marines and there was always a gap between the lines. The Army's 27th Division was pulled out of the lines and the Marine Corps 6th Division was put in there.

INT: *What was your job with the Marine Corps?*

ROY: I had a very important job. I was a PFC. I was a very frightened PFC. I mean, it's one thing to be a PFC, it's another thing to be scared shitless and be a PFC. So, I was in the second category. And I was a rifleman, nothing lower than just plain rifleman, and, uh, that was my job.

INT: *Your company didn't go north, you went south?*

ROY: That's right, we went south. By the time I got there, they were all through at the north and they were just going south. But the Shuri Naha Yonabaru Line—that was the big line the Japanese decided they were gonna make their stand there and not resist the landing. And the Marines couldn't believe that—the Japs actually decided they weren't gonna make a big resistance on the beach, that they were going to make it all on this southern tip. So, that's where all the fighting was.

INT: *Do you think they had learned, probably after all the islands, that they couldn't beat you guys on the beach, right?*

ROY: That's right. But they had designed their defense very intricate—this fire station would protect this one, and this one, and so on. They had interchangeable protection and it was very, very difficult to break that down. That's where they said, "We're going to make our stand here."

INT: *When did you guys realize that it wasn't going to be a cakewalk?*

ROY: When they took the backup Marines and put us in the lines with the original, the 1st Division was in the lines, and they put the 6th on the 1st Division's flank. That's when we knew, we're in for it now.

And the casualties were monumental. I mean, when the 6th was going up to the lines, we were going up in trucks and there were trucks on the other side coming back. There were Marines piled in those trucks, like cordwood, but you could always see the feet of the Marines. They put ponchos over 'em but the feet would be hanging out, so you could see all these feet dangling out. It was like a conveyor belt. We were going up on this side and they were coming back on that side—the only difference is that we were alive and they were dead. A minor difference.

INT: *That wasn't a good feeling, was it?*

ROY: No, it was not a good feeling. And if you were frightened to begin with, then you became very frightened. I wish I could tell you nice heroic stories, that I was a hero or something like that, but I wasn't. They call us lookie-loos [chuckles] where you're looking . . . oh, you're surprised. We were lookie-loos, we just looked.

INT: *What did you start running into?*

ROY: Then we had to get out of the trucks, of course, and walk the last couple miles up to the very front. Once we got to the front [pauses] ... it's an entirely different . . . It's just, uh . . . very different.

But, here's a story that shows the incongruity of the whole thing. For example, we were on the lines. This was after we went into the lines. The Marine Corps made a landing, another landing in back of the Japanese on the Oroku Peninsula.

But the 6th Marine Division made this landing in back because this Shuri Line was so difficult to break. So, the guys that do the big thinking said, "Well, the Japs are going to cave in if we land in back of them on this Oroku Peninsula."

They told my unit, "OK, now, the only landing craft we have are these [amphibious] amtracs." And there was a sea wall on Naha and they brought these amtracs alongside of the sea wall. And they told us, "OK, get in the amtrac, and you're going to go across. And as you have a straight line, one of the amtracs in the front will fire a flare, and then you all turn and go towards shore. And you're landing in back of the lines."

[dryly] That was exciting. Because as we're going across, the Japs were trying to put mortars into the amtracs, and you see this big splash alongside of you. . . .

[Roy Wilkes and the rest of the Marine 6th Division pushed into Naha, the Okinawan capital, in late May 1945, via an amphibious landing at an estuary below the city. Other American troops entered the capital by crossing the Asa- to River. By the first week of June 1945, Naha—a city of 75,000 people—was virtually deserted. Japanese pillboxes and other strong points had been overrun. With key bridg- es down, the destroyed city center and smashed railyard were effectively isolated. As the poorly trained Japanese defenders died or pulled back, they abandoned considerable amounts of ammunition and small arms. Fighting on the city's outskirts continued, but in the city proper, the main threat came from isolated Japanese snipers. Organized resistance across all of Okinawa ended on June 21.]

INT: **Tell me about how when they finally secured the island and called it off, what were you doing then?**

ROY: Well. What they did is, they said, "Hey, we're gonna secure the island today." We're on the southern tip already. They said, "They're gonna take some pictures about a mile away."
So we all decided to walk over there and see them secure

the island. So we walked about a mile and see this photographer with a whole bunch of guys with bayonets on their rifles. Our bayonets were all thrown away. That's the first thing you left on the ship.

[dryly] I said if I need my bayonet to kill a Jap, I'm gonna drown him in shit before that happens because I'm not heroic. You know, I'm not gonna get in a bayonet fight with anybody.

So anyway, we see this whole group of Marines that really looked rugged, and the photographer is saying, "I need a high point. I need like a little hill that these guys can get on." He's looking and he can't find a hill. And we're amused.

So then he's taking pictures and he says, "You guys, get in front there. We need you to fill out." So we got in front to fill out for the surrender on Okinawa pictures.

It was staged.

So maybe ten years after Okinawa, I see this picture of the surrender of Okinawa and I'm in it! I'm in the darn picture!

But anyway, the surrender and end of Okinawa was not that monumental. [Everybody was] just worn out because there was nobody left to kill.

[As Roy accurately remembered, however, Okinawa hadn't been entirely secured.]

Let me tell you, there was this big [cliff] drop-off and it was [full of] thousands of caves and the Marines were on the top and the Japanese wouldn't come out. They were too frightened to come out and the Marines were too frightened to go in.

There was this piece of Swiss cheese there, that's what the land looked like. The Japanese were in there. We tried everything to get them out. We tried smoke. We tried throwing grenades in. It was really a pain in the butt trying to get them out at the very end. Eventually we got them out. Not all of them, of course.

But then when we got on trucks to go back home, we couldn't believe it! We were just there a few weeks ago and there had been nothing. Now, there are Quonset huts as far as you can see! Quonset huts! Movie theaters! We said that we should have known that this was back here.

So the fight was going on at the very end . . . the rest of the island was secure and thriving, and eventually all the Japs gave up.

INT: **The U.S. command poured a lot of effort into Okinawa after the island was taken. But you went to Guam after the war, right?**

ROY: Yeah.

INT: **They were pouring everything into Okinawa because they thought that was going to be the main base.**

ROY: Yes. That was the main base for invading Japan. [Roy is referencing Operation Downfall, the U.S. plan for an amphibious invasion of the home islands of Japan, scheduled to begin in November 1945. But America's August 1945 atomic bombings of Hiroshima and Nagasaki meant that Downfall could be canceled—saving many hundreds of thousands of American and Japanese lives in the bargain.] So they were making that base [at Okinawa] when I left. They were putting up the Quonset huts and everything else they needed for the troops to come in there, but they never did use a lot of that.

INT: *So you went on to Guam after they secured Okinawa?*

ROY: Yes.

INT: *And you trained for the invasion of Japan?*

ROY: No. We went to Guam and thought we were going to go home now 'cuz America is going to reward its Marine Corps. So we got all of our sea bags packed, got on ships and we took off.

So after a couple days, we see land. We hear, "You're going to make a simulated battle landing at Tsingtao China." Why? They don't tell us. Like I said, the Marine Corps does not owe you an explanation. All they owe you is orders of what you're supposed to do and you could figure it out for yourself.

We hear, "We're going to make a simulated landing on China. Do not lock and load. There are friendlies ashore."

So we come to shore and sure enough the Chinese are really glad to see us because that means the Japanese are gonna go and they hated the Japs. They thought we were gonna be friendly. The Japs had been very hard on them.

So we get ashore and the rest is history.

INT: *One of the China stories you mentioned was that you were guarding coal mines or the trains with the Japanese? Tell me about that.*

ROY: Well, we got to the city Tsingtao and that's a pretty big city. It's got bars and . . . it's a city. So that wasn't bad duty.

[Note: Tsingtao, today known as Qingdao, is on the Chinese Yellow Sea coast, directly west of South Korea.]

But then they said, "Now you're gonna move." We're gonna get on a boat again and go [north] to Ching Wang Tao, a small village on the Manchurian border.

[Note: Chin Wang Tao is now known as Qinhuangdo.]

[Communist insurgent leader] Mao Tse-tung was in Manchuria and [Chinese Nationalist leader] Chiang Kai-shek was where we were. So the two of them were gonna have it out [for control of China] and we were gonna be like the referee. But there weren't enough of Chiang Kai-shek's troops [to secure the cities], so [U.S. command] took every [American] ship in the Pacific, sent it down south in China. They loaded Chiang Kai-shek [and his forces] on American

ships, hopscotched all of China.

Now, at the end of the war, Japan had occupied China—all the big cities, including Beijing [which was then] Peking. All occupied by Japanese. But the Japanese have now surrendered and they're not supposed to do anything.

So U.S. command took Chiang Kai-chek's men [from] the south and hopscotched China and brought them around to China's very northern part.

They said [to the Nationalists], "All right, you can now fight with Mao and now you're gonna occupy all of China. You're gonna go south."

They'd tell us, "Look, remember yesterday, the nice troops we saw from Chiang Kai-shek?" They were all nice and tan. Nice uniforms and so forth. Chinese get tan.

Well, the Nationalists went up into the hills and they sat down with the Communists and not a shot was fired. But they'd compare.

Communists: "How long are you in for?"
Nationalists: "Oh, we're in forever. We're in for life."
Communists: "Oh no, we're only in for three years."
Nationalists: "Yeah?"
Communists: "When did you get paid?"
Nationalists: "We don't get paid."
Communists: "Oh, we got paid six months ago."
Nationalists: "Wow! That's pretty good. You know what, we're gonna be Communists."

They turned their hats around and they're Communists without any firing, fighting, or anything.

And we're in the middle of this thinking this is not the way it's supposed to be working out.

What happened then is that Chang Kai-shek started his move to Formosa. Formosa is what we now call Taiwan, where the Chinese are. Big island, very well fortified.

[Note: During the war, Formosa was held by Japan. Following the Japanese surrender, an unenforceable U.S. assumption that the island would revert to mainland-Chinese control was undercut by the post-surrender presence on the island of Chiang's Nationalist troops, and the USA's willingness to regard Formosa as existing under Japanese sovereignty, an in-name-only status that did not officially end until the 1951 Japanese–Allied nations Treaty of San Francisco. The treaty took effect in 1952, three years after mainland China had fallen to Mao's Communist forces.]

So the Nationalists decided that Formosa was going to be their central point and they were gonna fight [Mao] from there.

And we thought they were gonna fight from the north where we're bringing them.

No. They looted the cities, brought it all to Formosa and then gave up. And that's how Mao took over China 'cuz Chiang Kai-shek just couldn't do it—couldn't hack it. The Marines were right in the middle of that.

[Note: Throughout the 1945-49 struggle for control of China, Mao gained an insurmountable advantage by rallying millions of people living in rural areas.]

INT: *So you were working side by side with Japanese troops?*

ROY: Oh, sure. We couldn't trust the Chinese and the Japanese just wanted to go home then. We were the Japanese ticket to home.

U.S. command couldn't trust the Chinese on the bridges. They could trust the Japs. So the Japs and the Marines guarded all the bridges 'cuz if the bridges went, they were up shit creek.

INT: *So in conclusion, being in the war must have been a pretty stressful situation there, wasn't it?*

ROY: It really was.

Once again, the noise because (sighs). . . you've got hundreds of howitzers—hundreds of them, and the shells coming in from the ships. So there's this constant firing and exploding. There's a sequence. It's a BOOM, with the howitzer being fired. Then errrr with the shell going overhead and then exploding.

After awhile you can tell when the shells are going overhead, whether it's incoming or outgoing, and whether they're near or far. If you've been there for awhile, certain shells coming doesn't bother you at all. But then if you say, "incoming" and yell and dive, that's gonna be close.

The sound is the thing that's crazy.

INT: *And I bet it was an awful good feeling when you knew it was over.*

ROY: Well, nobody told us, "Hey, it's over, we're all gonna be safe."

They didn't announce it.
They said, "Well, they're gonna secure the island."
That meant nothing to us, because it was make-believe. And it seemed—at least it seemed to me—you could still get killed when the island is secure. You could be the last one killed. I was constantly frightened. I never got over that.

INT: *I'm sure there were plenty of guys who probably got killed in the mop-up operation afterward?*

ROY: Oh, sure there were. But then you're frightened about, oh, where's the next battle going to be, are we going to go and hit Japan? Are we going to be the first in? I don't want that. So you're frightened about that.

INT: *There wasn't a whole lot of rejoicing because what was ahead was going to be even worse.*

ROY: Yeah. Going back to Guam, I was on the lieutenant's shit list because we were parked in this circle. And I don't know what the occasion, whether it was the 4th of July, or I don't know what it was. But I was on guard duty, still on guard duty, and I decided, "Hey, let's celebrate tonight.

Let's celebrate at 12 o'clock, let's all . . . fire. Celebrate 4th of July."

So everybody started firing. When you start firing, everybody who's asleep jumps up, grabs a rifle and goes out to the line, they got a spot out there and getting ready to—are they attacking, what's happening?

Lieutenant comes out. "OK, Wilkes, what's happening?"
"Oh, we heard the cans rattle, sir."
"And all of this because the cans are rattling, huh? Do you think you killed many of them out there, Wilkes?"
"I don't know, sir."
"Why don't you go out and see?"

Oh, you didn't want to do that because in the Marine Corps they have a saying that ten percent of the guys never get the word. In other words, you got to do something. There'll always be this ten percent that's like, "Huh, what are we doing now, I didn't know that."

So if I'm going to go out there on the wire, I know that ten percent of the guys aren't going to get the word that I'm out there and they're going to shoot me. I'm yellin', "Marine out on the wire! Marine out on the wire!" [laughs]

I went out there. They actually had me come back and say, "We didn't kill anybody, sir."
"Well, you're going to pay for this, Wilkes."

And when we left, we came back to Guam [in July, where the 6th Division remained until the end of September].

There had to be a group of men who were assigned to clean up the ship. I was one of them. So here finally, the battle's over for you, you come back, there's a Marine Corps band meeting the guys as they come off the ship. You don't come off the ship with them, you stay behind and work your ass off to clean the ship.

EPILOGUE

AFTER THE WAR

By

Elaine Wilkes,
Roy Wilkes' Daughter

What a ride!

MY DAD HUNG this quote on his office wall:

Life's journey is not to arrive at the grave safely
in a well-preserved body.
But rather to skid in sideways,
totally worn out, shouting,
"Holy shit . . . What a ride!"

And what a ride he had.

I don't know anyone who defied the odds like he did.

He had one foot in death's door probably over a dozen times.

It was Memorial Day, 1945. As a teenage Marine his platoon was advancing on enemy lines. Suddenly he heard an inner voice say, "Stop."

He stopped.

Seconds later a grenade went off killing more than twenty young Marines in front of him. He was in shock, buried to his chest with clouds of thick dust and death surrounding him. The Japanese were throwing shelling in the area to make sure everyone was killed.

Volunteer Marines ran in and pulled him out. Dazed, he walked back to the base, amidst the bombardment of shelling. Twice in one day—the explosion, and then bullets whizzing all around him—he defied the odds.

After the war ended, instead of going home he was assigned to guard Bridge #54 in Northeast China, and lived in a cold hut on barren land, without electricity, running water, heat, light, or telephone.

A year later he was finally discharged and sent back to the States. All the celebrations when the war ended were long over—and forgotten.
Not a parade in sight. No one to greet him. No hero's welcome. He was alone.

He was expected to pick up his life where he'd left it, as if the war had
never happened. No help with PTSD, which wasn't a recognizable trauma at the time.

Being on the front lines day after day, surrounded by death, fighting bloody battles, losing friends, and living in harsh conditions could make someone bitter.

Not Dad. He refused to feel sorry for himself.

Despite the inner battles that continued for the rest of his life, he focused on bettering himself.

Dad became a "self-made" man, and got me hooked on his countless audios on positive thinking, visualization, and success principles. These made a huge, lasting impact on my life. And so did his can-do attitude.

When I was twelve years old, we were driving on a family vacation. I looked out the car window and saw a swanky new hotel. My mom exclaimed, "The newspaper reported that hotel has a year-long waiting list. It's impossible to get a room there!"

Dad pulled the car over in the hotel's parking lot and said, "Wait here."

A couple minutes later he reappeared waving a hotel key for our "impossible to get" room.

How he'd do it?

After being told no rooms were available, Dad then went to the manager and asked, "If the President of the United States were to arrive tonight would you have a room for him?"

"Yes, of course," replied the manager.
Dad responded, "Great. I'll take his room and if he arrives, he can stay with me."

That night as we walked to our room, my dad turned to me and confided, "Remember: there's always room in the inn." Later I realized it was his way of showing, "Where there's a Wilkes, there's a way!"

Yes, he seemed to always find a way. He created a very successful business but remained humble. Over half of all small businesses fold by the end of the fifth year. Wilkes and McLean, the business he built from scratch, continues to be hugely successful after several decades. Again, Dad defied the odds.

Although this book describes the hell he went though, he was also lucky. Uncannily lucky. To him, slot machines were ATMs. Once while waiting to collect his winnings on a slot machine, he casually put money into the machine next to it and won there, too. Now waiting to be paid on two machines (heck, what else is there to do?), he put money into a third machine and won again—three slot machines in a row, all within a matter of minutes, each paying several thousand dollars. He did that repeatedly, even once scoring a $60,000 jackpot.
Badda bing badda boom!

But craps was his real game. He learned it in the Marines and then played the game for decades. He could calculate the odds faster than anyone there. His gambling philosophies mirrored his life: "Roll the dice and know it's all gonna be all right."

Another philosophy that mirrored life was, "Have a single-minded purpose. Simply focus on the game in the moment." He never obsessed about things that might not shake out exactly as he wanted. He was focused on being present in the game, rather than just focused on the outcome. I suspect he learned to be present during his time in the Marines.
Dad lived by "I reserve my mind for higher-level thinking." Maybe that's what helped him deal with numerous medical issues without going to the slums of his mind.

During surgery decades ago, a doctor ended a routine angioplasty and accidentally severing three of my father's arteries, forcing him into an emergency triple bypass surgery. Code Blue. Afterwards, Dad reported hovering over his body and watching eight people scurry to get him to emergency surgery. He made it—again.

Not once did I hear him say how angry he was at the doctor for putting him through this painful, unneeded triple bypass, or how unfair it was. Not a word. Instead he focused on recovering his health every day.

When he got out the hospital he'd muster enough energy to do one arm curl and mark it down in a ledger. The next day, two arm curls. Mark it down. Each day he would add more. Did he get this discipline from the Corps?

Through it all he kept his great personality and humor. Once, he said, "Elaine, the dietician came and talked to me. I'm going to start right away doing what she says to do."

I replied, "Oh, really, what did she say?"

He answered, "To drink more liquids . . . so bring me a Rob Roy cocktail."

He was funny and made things fun. He was also very patriotic. When we were kids, on Memorial day, the day he was wounded, and the 4th of July, he would turn the flag raising into a special family parade. We would all march in a straight line behind him as he carried the flag around the house singing the Marine Corps

Dad and me many years ago in Las Vegas, celebrating Memorial Day.

songs. Then he would place the flag in it's holder at the front door.

After we were all grown, he kept the U.S. flag and the Marine Corps flag up in his backyard every summer.

Later in life, when Dad was in rehab healing from back surgeries, the visiting doctor called the family into the meeting room and bluntly announced, "He's not going to make it."

In shock after catching my breath, I asked the doctor, "What makes you the soothsayer?"

He boldly replied, "I've been doing this for twenty-one years, and I'm a hundred percent sure he won't make it." At that he abruptly left.

We all were stunned by this experienced doctor's prediction. We went back into my dad's room and he asked, "What'd the doctor say?"

We were shell-shocked and not sure how to respond.

Dad looked at us confidently and said, "I'll make it."
And he did.

He ignored the doctor's certainty that he had zero-percent chance of living for the next three days. He ended up living several more years. What are the odds?

Even when he was on life support years later for MRSA, sepsis,

Even though many of Dad's yesterdays put him through hell, he always concentrated on how he could better his todays.

and kidney failure another doctor said, "It's unlikely he'll make it. You gotta be realistic." He didn't know Roy Wilkes. Dad not only made it, but again lived *years* longer.

Life threw him unbearable curveballs that would give many people proof how life was hell and had done them wrong. But through all his extreme hardships and nightmares and sleepless nights he had throughout his life, I never heard him complain, blame or feel sorry for himself. Instead, he chose to be resilient and focus on how to make the best of the situation. He appreciated how lucky he was to be alive—whatever the circumstance.

Maybe he wanted to live life to the fullest not only for himself, but for Bobbie and all his Marine buddies from Charlie Company who left us too soon.

Those buddies and angels were there to cheer him on with a hero's welcome when he skidded sideways into Heaven, totally worn out, shouting, "Holy shit! What a ride!"
Wanna know why I know he's in Heaven?
Because . . . there's always room in the inn . . . and . . .

where there's a Wilkes, there's a way.
Dad dying hurts so bad because having him in my life was so good.
He was my solid rock, voice of reason, buddy, and dad.

What an interesting life. God must have really loved him.

ACKNOWLEDGMENTS

By

Elaine Wilkes,
Roy Wilkes' Daughter

BECAUSE THIS BOOk was a labor of love, this wonderful team appeared and graced the book with their extraordinary talent. With immense gratitude to:

My mom, Ruth Wilkes, who went over every word of the book with me—numerous times! Her excellent suggestions and thoughtful discussions were a great help. Much love!

The brilliant editor with vast knowledge of WWII, David J. Hogan, who stayed true to my dad's words and polished a gem to make it super shiny. He is ah-mazing. *hogan949@gmail.com*

The wildly creative, wonderful artists who also were perfect for this book: Tuko, who created the awesome book cover that conveys the feelings of the book. *mayjendtetuko@gmail.com* and

I was beyond blessed to have Kevin Ong'any design the book's back cover, and interior. Like a wizard, he also made old pictures look new again. I'm amazed at his dedication to quality, work ethic, creativity, and how he made sure the book looked it's best. *artwanted.com/kevanovic, fliphtml5.com/bookcase/fnteg kevanovic@outlook.com*

My sounding boards: George Sobol, Karen Seeberg, and Alex Carroll who engaged me in discussions about titles, covers, ending, and more.

John Briggs, Major, United States Army (Retired), who acted as the military consultant and went over the book with great care and respect.

Elizabeth Amini, Connie Bishaf, Keith Bishaf, Lisa Chen, J.J. Coolio-Jack Jones, Judy Logue Gibbons, Robin Harlan, Cindy Leuty Jones, Rose Lane, Chris Walker, and Dave Zabowski who all gave their valuable input.

Thanks also to the people in several Facebook groups who took the time to vote on the covers and titles. That's so appreciated.

Bob Zimmerman, who allowed me to use an interview with my dad from his WWII documentary, Rise of the Valiant. *razfilms.com*

The U.S. Marine Corps history division—oral history branch, for giving me permission to use the interview with my dad.

The U.S. Marine Archives, for the use of the WWII images in the book, with corresponding picture captions from USMC Official Records.

Rock-solid book consultant David Aretha. *daretha@live.com*

And lastly, war is personal and generally has a lifelong impact on those who served, and on their families. God bless these families, my dad, and all of his Marine buddies.

Semper Fi.
Love, Elaine

BIOGRAPHY

Elaine Wilkes,
Roy Wilkes' Daughter

ELAINE WILKES is an internationally published author with *Hay House Publishers* and received the prestigious *Publishers Weekly* rare star recommendation. She also wrote and self-published several books, and is the recipient of six awards for her writings.

She has a Ph.D. in naturopathy, a master's degree in psychology, and certificates in many health fields, including nutrition.

Elaine has appeared as a holistic health expert on *CNN Headline News* and in publications such as the *Chicago Tribune, Huffington Post, Forbes, First for Women, Women's World*, and others.

She signed an exclusive acting contract with NBC, appeared on numerous television shows, and in over 70 TV commercials. Elaine was a season regular on the hit TV show *Dallas* and was in many movies. She has acted with many A-list actors such as Mark Harmon, Madonna, Courtney Cox, Bruce Willis, Billy Zane, Ted Danson, Larry Hagman, and others, and worked with legendary directors including John Hughes, Blake Edwards, and Joe Sedelmaier.

Elaine's websites are:

www.ElaineWilkes.com

www.aDateWithYourFuture.com

She also created Udemy.com online courses which have earned the prestigious "highest rated" badges by her students. One course is a modern, funny approach to the legendary *Think and Grow Rich* book. (A book her dad introduced her to when she was a teenager.) Two other courses are on how to use the iPhone's Siri as your personal assistant.

WAR IS PERSONAL

Made in the USA
Columbia, SC
13 January 2022

54241819R00102